THE *Incredible* POTATO COOKBOOK

Other cookbooks by Maria Luisa Scott and Jack Denton Scott
published by Consumer Reports Books

THE COMPLETE BOOK OF PASTA

RICE: A COOKBOOK

MASTERING MICROWAVE COOKING

THE BEAN, PEA & LENTIL COOKBOOK

THE *Incredible* POTATO COOKBOOK

Maria Luisa Scott
Jack Denton Scott
and the Editors of
Consumer Reports Books

CONSUMER REPORTS BOOKS
A DIVISION OF CONSUMERS UNION
Yonkers, New York

Published by Consumers Union of United States, Inc.,
Yonkers, New York 10703.

Library of Congress Cataloging-in-Publication Data

Scott, Maria Luisa.
The incredible potato cookbook / Maria Luisa Scott, Jack Denton Scott,
and the editors of Consumer Reports Books.
p. cm.
Includes index.
ISBN 0-89043-456-5
1. Cookery (Potatoes) 2. Potatoes. I. Scott, Jack Denton, 1915— .
II. Consumer Reports Books. III. Title.
TX803.P8S37 1991
641.6′521—dc20 *91-38274*
CIP

Design by Ruth Kolbert
Second printing, August 1992
Manufactured in the United States of America

The Incredible Potato Cookbook is a Consumer Reports Book published by Consumers Union, the nonprofit organization that publishes *Consumer Reports,* the monthly magazine of test reports, product Ratings, and buying guidance. Established in 1936, Consumers Union is chartered under the Not-for-Profit Corporation Law of the State of New York.

The purposes of Consumers Union, as stated in its charter, are to provide consumers with information and counsel on consumer goods and services, to give information on all matters relating to the expenditure of the family income, and to initiate and to cooperate with individual and group efforts seeking to create and maintain decent living standards.

Consumers Union derives its income solely from the sale of *Consumer Reports* and other publications. In addition, expenses of occasional public service efforts may be met, in part, by nonrestrictive, noncommercial contributions, grants, and fees. Consumers Union accepts no advertising or product samples and is not beholden in any way to any commercial interest. Its Ratings and reports are solely for the use of the readers of its publications. Neither the Ratings, nor the reports, nor any Consumers Union publications, including this book, may be used in advertising or for any commercial purpose. Consumers Union will take all steps open to it to prevent such uses of its material, its name, or the name of *Consumer Reports.*

ACKNOWLEDGMENT

Our warm thanks to our editor, Julie Henderson,
who has given our book strength and clarity
because of her talented know-how.

Contents

THE *Incredible* POTATO COOKBOOK

Introduction

ALL ABOUT POTATOES

Americans eat four times more potatoes than any other vegetable. The potato also appears on menus more often than any other single food. And no one can deny that the potato may be our best food buy—an economical, savory stand-in for meat.

Yet many of us still consider this important vegetable to be a fattening filler, long on starch, fat, and carbohydrates and indulged in only at the risk of expanding our waistlines. But let's look at the facts:

- You would have to eat 11 pounds of potatoes to put on 1 pound of weight.
- Americans spend only 2 percent of their food dollar on potatoes but receive more than 25 percent of their energy and nutrient requirements from them.
- Potatoes provide 74.5 percent more food energy per acre than wheat and 77.6 percent higher protein per acre than rice.

- The potato contains only 1 percent fat. Ounce for ounce it has no more calories than an apple and is less caloric than equal weights of avocados and equivalent portions of rice or bran flakes.
- If our entire daily diet consisted of potatoes, we would get all our required riboflavin (vitamin B2), one and a half times our iron, three to four times our thiamine (vitamin B1) and niacin (vitamin B3), and more than ten times the amount of vitamin C we need for a healthy diet. (U.S. Department of Agriculture statistics).

THE HISTORICAL POTATO

The Incas of Peru first cultivated the potato around 200 B.C. In 1537, a scouting party of Spanish conquistadores entered the deserted Andean village of Sorocota. Looking for food, they found corn, beans, and a strange rootlike vegetable that came in various sizes and ranged in color from gold and red to black, blue, and gray.

The Spanish discovered that the vegetable had many medicinal uses for the Incas—raw slices were placed on broken bones, rubbed on the head to cure aches, used as heat retainers to relieve the pain of arthritis and gout, or rubbed on the face and body to cure skin disorders. The Incas also ate slices with other foods to prevent indigestion. But the root was most highly prized as a food staple. The conquistadores found it to be "floury, of good flavor, a dainty dish even for Spaniards."

The Incas called the miracle plant that came in so many varieties *papa,* meaning tuber. The Spaniards chose to call it *turma de tierra,* or truffle. Today Spanish-speaking people call the vegetable by its original Inca name or sometimes *patata;* the English "potato" is a corruption of *batata,* West Indian for sweet potato.

The Spaniards also were intrigued to find that the Incas had learned to preserve the vegetable almost indefinitely. The Indians were in the habit of taking the potatoes high up into the Andes, leaving them to freeze at night and thaw in the sunlight. Eventually the potatoes became hard and lightweight. Sometimes they cooked and cut up the potatoes before beginning the freeze-and-drying process; at other times they eliminated the moisture in the potatoes by stamping and crushing them with their bare feet. They called the world's first freeze-dried food *chuno.*

The potato was brought to Europe sometime later. Both Sir Walter Raleigh and Sir Francis Drake are given the credit, but reason and the facts give the edge to the conquistadores, particularly a Spanish monk, Hierinynus Cardan. Unfortunately, the potato became an object of disdain, which halted its early spread as a valuable food crop in Europe. The reasons stemmed from the superstitions of the day—for example, the potato was not mentioned in the Bible, thus was unfit for human consumption; the potato was a member of the "dangerous" nightshade family; the potato was not grown from seed so it was said to be evil and perhaps responsible for the diseases of leprosy, syphilis, and scrofula. As late as the eighteenth century, Russian peasants preferred to starve rather than plant and eat the "unclean" potato.

Finally, the economical and nutritional value of the potato became so evident that in 1744, Frederick II of Germany ordered his peasants to plant the vegetable, under penalty of imprisonment. In 1764, a royal edict forced Swedish farmers to grow potatoes on their land.

In France, the pharmacist Antoine Parmentier, who learned to enjoy potatoes when he was a prisoner of the Germans during the Seven Years War, invited the powerful of the day (including Benjamin Franklin) to his home, where he offered them an all-potato menu. He also used subtle psychology to persuade French farmers to plant the vegetable. King Louis XVI had given him permission to plant potatoes at Les Sablons, a sandy, barren stretch of land near Paris. During the day Parmentier stationed soldiers to stand guard at the potato field, but at night the guard was removed. Curious about the "valuable" crop, farmers living nearby stole a number of the plants at night and put them in their own gardens. The rest is history. Today, France honors Parmentier by naming some of their best potato dishes after him.

England did not produce potatoes in any quantity until 1796. Earlier, in 1663, England had sent potatoes to Ireland, where they eventually became that nation's main food source. Prior to the disastrous potato famine of the 1840s, when the country's entire crop was decimated by the potato blight, the majority of the Irish lived on potatoes and milk (it is said that many adults consumed from 8 to 10 pounds of potatoes a day).

In 1719, a colony of Irish settled at Londonderry, New Hampshire. They brought the potato with them and planted it on their land. The vegetable was slow to win favor in the colonies, however, until some members of the local aristocracy pronounced them quite palatable and tasty and made a point of serving them regularly at meals.

THE NUTRITIONAL POTATO

It is only recently that global nutritionists began to appreciate the many virtues of the potato and its value as an important dietary staple in more than 130 countries. This common vegetable is a valuable source of protein—a medium-size potato supplies 2.1 grams of good-quality protein. It's also high in potassium, a necessary element for maintaining the body's electrolyte balance. In addition, the potato contains magnesium, phosphorous, calcium, copper, and other important minerals. Its sodium level is only about 3 milligrams, which makes it a valuable food in low-sodium diets. Its supply of carbohydrate is 92 to 98 percent usable by the body; its supply of iron is 93 percent usable; its vitamin B is more usable by the body than a similar amount of purified, isolated vitamin B itself.

The potato is such a near-perfect food, in fact, that the agricultural research arm of the U.S. Department of Agriculture has stated that "a diet of whole milk and potatoes would supply almost all of the food elements necessary for the maintenance of the human body."

THE CALORIC POTATO?

Dr. Jean Mayer of Tufts University, a onetime Presidential adviser on nutrition, insists that people are wrong when they claim that starchy foods like the potato are fattening. The fact is the potato has fewer calories than many other foods—about 110 calories in a 150-gram, medium-size potato.

Nutritionist R. A. Seelig remarked that when starch is substituted for sugar in the diet, the appetite actually decreases. For this reason, and also because potatoes supply many vitamins and minerals, people should include them in any kind of reducing diet.

Not long ago, a Michigan State graduate student put the potato to a calorie test. For 22 days, he ate 4 pounds of potatoes a day. He boiled them for breakfast, made potato salads for lunch, and cooked home fries for dinner. No matter how he prepared them, his consumption of potatoes came to only 1,300 calories a day. To increase his caloric intake, the student added extra fats in the form of butter, cream, and cheese to his diet. At the end of the three-week potato diet, he had put on exactly four ounces. From this test and from scientific observation about the merits of the potato, it's clear that the potato is a much-maligned victim of America's ongoing obsession with calories and dieting.

Not so, say others. People add fatty items such as butter, sour cream, and gravies to their mashed and baked potatoes, so the calories do add up. Certainly the addition of these extra ingredients won't help anyone lose weight, but they do supply extra calcium and vitamin A to the diet. Assuming you don't load up on other high-calorie or fattening foods, potatoes make a superb nutritional base to which can be added other nutrients needed by the body.

See the calorie comparison table that clarifies the role of the potato in the diet on page 7.

THE CULTIVATABLE POTATO

Potatoes may not only be one of the world's most perfect foods, but they are also one of the easiest to grow. We have always found raising potatoes an enjoyable and rewarding task. It's difficult to define the personal pleasure received from digging up potatoes you've planted yourself and feeling them firm in your hands, smelling of the good earth, with an almost pungent yet exciting and seldom-experienced aroma that above-the-earth vegetables do not have. Another bonus is the fecundity of the potato, which from a small cut-out piece with two or three "eyes" can produce a whole cluster of offspring.

There is one drawback, however. They do need room. To supply enough potatoes for the needs of one person requires 70 to 100 feet. If you can supply the land, then you should know that potatoes like somewhat sandy, light soil, and should be planted about May 1 on the East Coast.

CALORIE COMPARISONS

	CALORIES
POTATOES, boiled, ½ cup	45
mashed, milk added	70
baked, 1 medium, ½ cup	90
potato salad with dressing, ½ cup	99
Spaghetti, cooked, ¾ cup	115
Bread, 2 slices	120
Whiskey, 100 proof, 1 jigger	125
Biscuit, one, 2½ inches in diameter	130
Candy, chocolate, 1-ounce bar	150
Rice, cooked, ¾ cup	150
Sweet potato, baked, 1 medium	155
Milk, whole, one 8-ounce glass	165
Peanuts, roasted, 1 ounce	170
Pancakes, three, 4 inches in diameter	180
Pizza, ⅛ a 14-inch pie	180
Macaroni, with cheese, ½ cup	240
Ground beef, 3-ounce patty, cooked	245
Steak, 4 × 2½ × ½ inch	330
Cake, chocolate, 2-inch section of 10-inch layer cake	420
Milk shake, 12 ounces	520

Check with local gardeners to find out the exact planting date for your locale.

What variety do you want to grow? We always plant the Russet Burbank, which is the mealy Idaho. They don't have quite the genuine Idaho flavor, imparted by the soil in Idaho, but they are superb. (Descriptions of other varieties follow later in this chapter.)

After you decide which variety you want, make sure to buy "certified" seed stock from your local garden center or from a seed company. Certified assures you that they are guaranteed to produce and have not been chemically sprayed to stop sprouting. Seed potatoes are sold by the pound. Three pounds are sufficient for a 25-foot long row.

The first step is to cut the seed potatoes into sections, each containing two eyes. We use three (an extra one is for good luck). When you put them into the soil make sure one eye is staring upward at you, more or less centered in the planting hole. They should be planted 12 inches apart, 5 inches deep, in rows 30 inches apart.

After the plants begin sprouting, in about 2 weeks, cultivate them weekly. Hoe out the weeds and build hills around each plant, using the soil from the walking area between the rows. This "hilling" will protect the growing potatoes from too much sun, which turns them green and gives them a bitter taste.

When the plants are 12 inches high they begin bearing blossoms. This is the signal to start spreading bone meal, compost, or manure once around each hill. Don't overdo it though, or the potatoes may pick up a disease known as the common scab. One bushel of manure for every 100 feet is a safe limit.

If the season is dry, water the plants well once a week—in the morning. This gives the foliage a chance to dry out during the day and prevents rotting, especially if you've watered the leaves more than the thirsty tubers underground can manage to absorb.

When do you harvest? Easy. Begin harvesting when the plants become very dry and start to tumble over. This should occur in early fall, about four months after the seed stock was planted. (Make sure you finish harvesting before the first frost.) Two weeks after the plants become dry, pull them up and dig out the potatoes.

Each plant should contain a crop of several potatoes in about an 8-inch layer. Don't, however, just start digging aimlessly or you'll end up spearing the potatoes with your spade. Begin from the outside edge, carefully digging straight down. Bring up the potato crop in sections. Then carefully turn the soil over and pick out the potatoes.

If you don't have the space, time, or inclination to raise your own potatoes, don't feel cheated. Good potatoes are available in most supermarkets. Not only are they among the best of all food buys, but they come in a wide variety of shapes, sizes, and textures.

THE VERSATILE POTATO

Americans may mistakenly consider the potato fattening, but we eat a lot of them, and in varied and interesting ways. We have created more potato stuffings than any other country, from cottage cheese and sour cream to caviar and salmon. We also hash, mash, mince, cream, dry, steam, boil, and roast potatoes; we add them to soups and chowders; we combine them with cheese, onions, butter, and milk as a main dish; we team them with tuna and chicken; we make potato croquettes; we pair potatoes with meat in pies; and we use them in casseroles and stews. Yes, we even make delicious doughnuts and cakes with potatoes (see the chapter on sweets).

The French, who call the potato *pomme de terre* or "apple of the earth," are not far behind us. They have over 100 classic potato recipes, including potato puffs, the impressive *pommes Anna*—potatoes sliced very thin, baked, and turned out like a cake—to the ubiquitous and world-famous "French fries."

But it's the Germans who may respect the potato the most. They have two names for the vegetable—*kartoffel* or truffle, and *erdapfel,* earth apple. They use it imaginatively in noodles, dumplings, pancakes, and breads. They also mix mashed potatoes with applesauce, sugar, and vinegar, and stuff poultry with the mixture. Their hot potato salad is world famous.

In Russia and Poland, the potato is the base for many hearty soups. It's also stewed in sour cream, filled with spicy mushrooms, included in classic main dish puddings, and used as a stuffing with meat and fish.

The Italians turn the *patate* into their famous dish *gnocchi,* the Spanish use the potato in a spectacular omelet, and the Swiss have created a national potato dish called *roesti,* which is a flat potato cake.

The ways of the world with the poor person's mainstay and the gourmet's delight are endless and fascinating. They are the reasons for this book. Here is a balanced collection of representative and respected potato recipes from around the globe. Here are the classic, the familiar, the famous, as well as the little known, the innovative, and the ingenious. In short, here is the incredible potato in all its glory.

1

Potato Techniques, Tips, and Varieties

VARIETIES OF POTATOES

Although potatoes are given different names in various parts of the country, there are basically four types: Russet, Long White, Round Red, and Round White. Each of these comes in several varieties, and each has its own champions. For example, some people believe that the best Long Whites come from eastern Long Island. Californians disagree; they also have a famous Long White. Many think that the best Russet is that mealy mouthful from Idaho. People in Maine don't agree—they also have a famed Russet baker. Perhaps the most popular Russet of all is the Russet Burbank. The Norland and the Red Pontiac are favored in the Round Reds; in the Round Whites are found the Superior and the Katahdin.

Contrary to what many of us believe, new potatoes are not a variety in themselves. All types of potatoes can be bought as "new" potatoes early enough in the season, but the timing of their appearance varies regionally. These thin-skinned tasty little morsels come to the market directly from the field and are not placed in storage. They are harvested as small, tender potatoes with a unique, feathery skin texture. Usually, they are available all year round in limited quantities. New potatoes are excellent boiled, steamed, or in salads.

Round Reds are best for oven roasting or boiling; Round Whites and Long Whites are fine for mashing, frying, boiling, and roasting. Both Whites are good for salads. Russets are the classic bakers, the fluffiest and mealiest. But there are those (including the authors) who believe that the Russets from Idaho can be used for anything. They are excellent for potato dumplings and pancakes, also for *gnocchi* and French fries. We also like the Russets baked for 4 minutes in the microwave oven, then peeled and sliced to make steak or country fries.

A good rule of thumb: Bakers are mealy and dry; boilers are moist and firm.

Generally, we do not specify the variety of potato to use in the recipes that follow. If you want to know what kind of potato is best for a salad or for French fries, you can always refer back to this section. After all, most people have a favorite all-purpose variety and we don't want to upset that potato cart. For instance, few of us are such perfectionists that we will complain about a salad because the potatoes have a mealy texture rather than the firm and waxy texture that experts claim is better.

BUYING AND STORING POTATOES

The grading of potatoes is on a voluntary basis, except where it is required by state law or by a Federal Marketing order. The best is U.S. Extra No. 1, which means the potatoes weigh 5 ounces, are 2¼ inches in diameter, and have no visible defects. The next grade, the U.S. No. 1, must be 1⅞ inches in diameter with no minimum size.

Choose loose potatoes that are well formed, smooth, and firm, with few or no eyes, and no discoloration, cracks, bruises, or soft spots. Firmness is especially important. Red potatoes and some whites are sometimes treated with colored or clear wax to make them appear fresher than they are. Avoid them. The FDA requires that these potatoes be plainly marked, but you can spot them by their unnatural waxy feel. Do not buy potatoes that have even the slightest greenish hue, which results from being overexposed to light. They have a bitter, unpleasant flavor and can be poisonous if eaten in large quantities.

Do not wash potatoes before storing, as this hastens decay. Store them in a dry, dark place at 45° to 50°F. If they are firm and reasonably fresh when purchased they will last up to three months. If you must store them at warmer temperatures, buy only a week's supply at a time. Higher temperatures cause fast sprouting and shriveling.

Do not store potatoes in the refrigerator. Below 40°, potato starch turns to sugar, making the potato much too sweet. Too-cold storage also causes the potatoes to darken during cooking.

COOKING TIPS

Nutrients found close to the skin are lost when potatoes are peeled before cooking. Therefore, for full nutritional value you should bake, boil, or steam potatoes in their skins. If you must peel them for cooking, use a vegetable parer and peel as thinly as possible.

Although it is advisable to cook potatoes in their skins, we are not necessarily going to stress this point in each recipe unless it makes a difference to that particular dish. For example, the French rarely cook potatoes in the skins. So, for a classic French dish, we stick with the authenticity of the recipe and peel the potatoes beforehand. If the recipe specifically calls for potatoes cooked in their skins, we usually state that, too. If we do not mention it at all, and if it is possible for you to boil and steam the potatoes in their skins, by all means do so.

A few more potato tips: Don't fret if you find you've oversalted or overspiced soups, stews, or main dishes. Simply add cut-up raw potatoes to the dish as it cooks; it will absorb some of the excess overflavoring. Tame the game bird, too, by adding diced potatoes, alone or in combination with onion, apple, or celery, to the bird's cavity. It will absorb some of the "gamey" flavor. Or add a bay leaf or your favorite herb to the water in which you boil potatoes—the flavored water can then be used to advantage in soups, stews, and gravies. The water can also be used instead of milk for making mashed potatoes.

POTATO EQUIVALENTS

1 POUND POTATOES EQUALS:

3 medium-size
3 cups peeled and sliced
2½ cups peeled and diced
2 cups mashed
2 cups French fries
2 cups grated

2 POUNDS MEDIUM POTATOES EQUALS:

6 servings potato salad, averaging 1 potato per serving

POTATO COOKING TECHNIQUES

To Boil In a heavy saucepan with a tight-fitting lid, cook the potatoes in about 1 inch of boiling salted water until fork tender. If they are whole, cook 30 to 40 minutes; cut up, 20 to 25 minutes. (The water may boil off if the lid doesn't fit tightly, so check occasionally and add more hot water if necessary.)

To Bake A medium-size potato will bake in 45 minutes to an hour at 400°F. However, oven temperatures can range from 325°F to 450°F, so you can bake the potatoes along with whatever else you have in the oven, thus saving energy. Adjust the timing according to the temperature.

Pierce the skin of each potato in several places with a fork before baking to allow the steam to escape and prevent the potato from bursting. Bake directly on the oven rack or on a baking sheet. Potatoes are done when they test soft when pinched with mitted hands or when easily pierced with a slim skewer or fork. If soft skins are desired, rub each potato with a little salad oil before baking.

To Mash Prepare boiled or steamed potatoes; drain and peel. (You can peel the potatoes beforehand, but then some of the nutrients are lost in the water. Besides, the skins of hot boiled potatoes slip off easily.) Using a potato masher, electric mixer, or ricer, mash the potatoes. Gradually add some milk, salt and pepper to taste, and, if you like, a pat or two of butter or margarine. Beat until the potatoes are light and fluffy. The texture of the potatoes will depend on the amount of milk used; the more milk, the creamier and thinner the potatoes. Too much milk will make them thin and soupy.

Consistency also depends on how you mash the potatoes. An electric mixer gives a smooth purée, while mashing by hand may leave some lumps but usually results in a fluffier, more "substantial" taste and texture. In any case, do not overprocess if you use an electric beater.

To Pan Roast Prepare boiled or steamed potatoes, but cook only 10 minutes; drain and peel. Arrange the potatoes in a shallow pan. Brush with melted butter, margarine, or salad oil. Bake, uncovered, at 400°F, or until fork tender, turning occasionally and basting. If roasting with meat, arrange peeled, raw, halved or quartered potatoes around the meat in the roasting pan about 1½ hours before serving. Baste with pan drippings. Turn and baste frequently to brown.

To Steam This is one of the most effective ways to preserve the nutrients in the potato. If you don't have a steamer, you can improvise by placing a wire rack on the bottom of a kettle or large saucepan and adding water to just below the level of the rack. Bring the water to a boil, put the potatoes on the rack, and cook over medium heat, tightly covered, until fork tender: whole, 30 to 45 minutes; cut up, 20 to 30 minutes. If the lid doesn't fit tightly, check occasionally and add more hot water, if necessary. If you don't have a rack, invert custard cups or crumpled aluminum foil to make an elevated platform on which the potatoes can be placed.

To Rice Prepare boiled or steamed potatoes, drain, and peel. Force the potatoes through a potato ricer or food mill. They may be tossed with a little melted butter or margarine before or after ricing.

To French Fry Cut raw peeled potatoes into strips about ¼ to ½ inch thick. Toss the strips into a bowl of ice water to keep crisp while cutting the remainder. Don't soak too long, since the potatoes will lose nutrients and absorb water, thus prolonging the cooking time and making the potatoes oily and soggy.

Pat the strips thoroughly dry with paper towels. Heat about 4 inches of vegetable oil to 390°F in a deep-fat fryer or large heavy saucepan. Place a layer of potato strips in a wire basket and immerse the basket in the hot fat; or place the strips, a few at a time, directly in the hot oil. Cook about 5 minutes, or until golden brown and tender. Drain well on paper towels; salt lightly and keep warm in a 300°F oven until ready to serve.

To Prepare Potatoes for a Salad It is best to use potatoes with a firm, waxy texture in salads; new potatoes are best, but Round Whites or Reds are also excellent. For salads, cook the potatoes in their skins to retain most of their flavor. Salads are also much tastier if the potatoes are peeled hot and the salad dressing added while the slices are still warm.

Microwave Cooking It is one of the marvels of the microwave oven that it can bake a 7-ounce potato in 4 minutes. This speed is in contrast to an electric or gas oven that takes 45 minutes to an hour. The savings in energy is impressive, but so is the fact that having a baked potato for dinner can be a last-minute decision.

To microwave, select 7-ounce, blocklike potatoes that are uniform in size. If the potatoes are too tapered, the slender portion will be cooked before the bulk of the potato. Similarly, if you cook small and large potatoes together, the smaller ones will be done first. Scrub the potatoes and pierce them in several places with a sharp knife on both sides. If you are cooking one potato, place it in the center of the oven. If more than one (do not cook more than six at a time), place the potatoes in a spokelike fashion, at least 1 inch apart.

It isn't necessary to place the potatoes on a dish. Cook

them on double-folded paper toweling. The towels will absorb some of the moisture from the potatoes and prevent oversteaming.

Cooking time, as with all food in the microwave oven, depends upon the size and variety of potato. We have found that a Maine or New York State potato cooks more quickly than the more solid Idaho. **Caution:** When half of the cooking time has elapsed turn over the potato. When we cook a 7-ounce potato for 4 minutes, we set the timer on 2 minutes as a reminder, then turn it and cook it another 2 minutes. Each cook must experiment with the timing of the oven (and the type of potatoes) to cook a potato to his or her own taste satisfaction.

MICROWAVE BAKING TIME FOR A 7-OUNCE POTATO

1 potato	4 to 5 minutes
2 potatoes	6 to 7 minutes
3 potatoes	8 to 9 minutes
4 potatoes	10 to 11 minutes
6 potatoes	14 to 15 minutes

When cooking in the microwave oven, remember that the *carry-over cooking time* is important. We always remove potatoes when they are still rather firm, and allow for the carry-over time to finish the cooking. If potatoes look withered before you remove them from the oven, they are overcooked. Don't be discouraged—trial and error will perfect your timing.

If preparing a simple baked potato, cook the full 4 minutes. But if baking a potato for further cooking, cut some time, looking ahead to the additional cooking that will be necessary. For example, if you are going to hash-brown potatoes later, reduce the cooking time of a 4-minute potato to 3½ minutes.

In microwave potato cooking, baking the potato is first. Then, using a browning skillet, you can transform that baked potato into cottage, country, steak-fried, scalloped, or hash brown potatoes, or chopped into a hot potato salad or a creamed potato dish.

Just remember, when adapting recipes from conventional cooking, the microwave oven cooks in about one-fourth the time. Always remember to allow for carry-over cooking time which, in microwave cookery, is accentuated.

We have found no advantage in using the microwave oven for boiling or steaming potatoes.

PROCESSED POTATOES

Potatoes are so popular, and so much in demand as a meal staple, that food processors have come up with many ingenious ways to precook and package the vegetable. Numerous appealing, easy-to-prepare potato products are now found on grocery shelves, a boon to busy homemakers and cooks.

Of course, the real thing is always preferable to the dehydrated, instant variety, but when time is short the commercially prepared potato can make a surprisingly good side dish. We were served crusty, tasty hash brown potatoes with a delectable beef pot roast at a friend's home recently. We both remarked on the excellent potatoes, and how expertly our hostess managed to get them just right, never an easy task with hash browns. Our hostess smiled and thanked us. A few days later, in a telephone conversation, she told us that the hash browns were dehydrated and came out of a box.

So, armed with that experience and our samplings of other types of processed potatoes, it's our opinion that the dehydrated variety have come a long way in a short time and busy people today should not have any qualms about serving them in a pinch.

All processed potatoes carry instructions and cooking suggestions on their packages, but here are a few more thoughts on preparing them, plus some ideas to stir your culinary imagination.

Dehydrated instant flakes make mashed potatoes, potato patties, Chantilly and Duchess potatoes, soup rosettes and other decorative trim, *gnocchi,* vichyssoise, soufflés, or cheese puffs. Use in any recipe that calls for mashed potatoes, or use directly from the package when thickening gravies or sauces, for breading, biscuits, pancakes, doughnuts, or quick and yeast breads.

Dehydrated diced potatoes make home-fries, hash browns, O'Brien potatoes. Use in casseroles, salads, soups, or chowders. Cream or prepare for scalloped or au gratin potato dishes.

Dehydrated shredded potatoes make hash browns, potato pancakes, potato bread. Extends and keeps meat loaf and meatballs moist and tender.

Dehydrated scalloped with sauce makes Delmonico potatoes or hot German potato salad. Use in casseroles or add to any combination of meat, fish, or fowl.

Dehydrated au gratin with sauce is used in casserole combinations.

Canned small whole peeled potatoes are useful in stews or for every kind of fried or roasted potato dish.

Frozen French fries come in various cuts: straight, crinkle, thin, shoestrings, or wedge. Use in casseroles or as a side dish or snack.

Frozen hash browns, Southern style, or shredded are useful as home fries, hash browns, or for O'Brien potatoes. Also useful in casseroles, as creamed, scalloped, or au gratin potatoes.

Frozen potato rounds (tots, logs, gems) make suitable side dishes or snacks.

Frozen cottage fries make every style of fried potato. Use for scalloped and au gratin dishes or for casseroles.

Frozen patties (triangles, round) are served fried or grilled or used as a base for open-faced broiled sandwiches.

Frozen small whole peeled are useful in stews, roasted, or heated and served with lemon butter, parsley, or chives.

As with the baked potato, you can find many new uses for the processed potato. Some suggestions:

- Use instant mashed potatoes to make baked eggs in potato nests, as a cover for a stew or casserole, or as a base for creamed dishes.
- Make an interesting potato and chicken or turkey loaf with frozen hash browns and crinkle-cut French fries. Mix the hash browns with cooked chopped meat, along with onion, seasonings, and milk—line the loaf pan with the fries, then pour in the meat mixture and bake.
- Use crushed potato chips instead of bread crumbs when dredging seafood or chicken.
- Use potato sticks to top creamed dishes.
- Dip chicken in beaten egg and then in instant potato flakes before baking or frying.
- Cover a casserole with potato "tots" during the last 15 minutes of baking time.
- Use shredded hash browns as a base for potato pancakes.

- Cook frozen French fries and serve as an appetizer with guacamole or hummus.
- Top country fries with creamed fish or chicken.

As you can see, the ways with processed potatoes are many and varied. In fact, new potato products are coming out so fast that it's difficult to keep up with them. Included are thick, steak-cut French fries, thick-sliced cottage fries, stuffed baked potato puffs, mashed potato balls, potatoes in many types of sauces. Some of these products come in convenient "no-clean-up" plastic cooking pouches. All are handy to use when time is short and starting from the raw potato just isn't possible.

There's no question that the Incas, who first developed the potato and learned to preserve it, would understand and accept these latest transformations. They have probably turned over in their graves—with envy.

Chicken Broth

Since a number of recipes in this book call for chicken broth, it is appropriate here to offer our own recipe.

A number of good commercial chicken broths are on the market (some low-sodium, which we recommend), but there is nothing like your own, simmered until it is as rich as you like it, then strained and used immediately, or frozen for later use. Some of the broth can be frozen along with nuggets of the chicken meat picked from the bones to produce any number of future quick, delicious soups.

4 pounds chicken backs, wings, and necks
4 quarts water
2 medium-size onions, each studded with 2 whole cloves

2 large celery stalks with leaves, coarsely chopped
2 medium-size carrots, scraped and coarsely chopped
6 sprigs broadleaf parsley
2 small bay leaves
¼ teaspoon dried thyme
8 black peppercorns, slightly crushed
1 teaspoon salt

1. Place all ingredients in a large soup pot. Cover and bring to a boil. Reduce heat to low and simmer for 30 minutes, skimming off surface foam as necessary.
2. Remove the cover and, at a bare simmer, cook for 2 hours, or until the liquid is reduced by half. Taste for seasoning.
3. Discard all vegetables. Save the chicken meat for soups. Strain the broth into a large bowl, and store in the refrigerator overnight. Sediment will settle to the bottom, fat will solidify on top.
4. Carefully remove the fat and discard. Spoon the clear, jellied broth into another bowl. Discard the sediment remaining in the first large bowl.

MAKES ABOUT 2 QUARTS

ALCOHOL

Depending on cooking time and temperature, between 5 percent and 85 percent of the alcohol used in the recipes in this book evaporates during cooking. However, we have made the inclusion of alcohol optional in most of these recipes.

Soups

SOUP AND POTATOES ARE A NATURAL COMBINATION, WITH THE potato acting as an enhancer, an emulsifier, and a blender of flavors. But such is the magic of the potato that its own personality is never lost, no matter what the other ingredients.

For example, clam chowder would not be the tasty and robust soup that it is without potatoes, and the French *garbure* would be an undistinguished medley without the potato to bind it all together. Potatoes produce the velvety classic vichyssoise, as well as a simple but very tasty mashed potato soup. And can you imagine a leek soup without the potato?

Central American Potato Soup with Chicken and Pumpkin

There's no adequate substitute for the pumpkin in this recipe. So plan to serve it when pumpkins are available.

3 tablespoons butter or margarine
1 medium-size onion, chopped
1 garlic clove, minced
1 teaspoon salt
½ teaspoon ground coriander
½ teaspoon ground allspice
1 bay leaf
4 cups Chicken Broth (page 22), or canned
2 cups ½-inch cubes fresh pumpkin (1¼ pounds)
4 large potatoes (1½ pounds), peeled and cut into ½-inch cubes
Pinch of red pepper flakes
2 cups cubed cooked chicken (1 pound)
2 tablespoons chopped fresh coriander or parsley

1. In a large pot, melt the butter or margarine. Add the onion and garlic and cook for 2 minutes. Stir in the salt, ground coriander and allspice, and bay leaf.
2. Add the chicken broth, pumpkin and potato cubes, and red pepper flakes. Bring to a boil. Simmer for 15 minutes, or until the potatoes and pumpkin are tender but still firm. Taste for seasoning.
3. Add the chicken and simmer until heated through. Remove the bay leaf.
4. Sprinkle the fresh coriander or parsley on top of individual servings.

MAKES 9 1/2 CUPS, TO SERVE 6

Potato and Cheese Soup

3 tablespoons butter or margarine
1 medium-size white onion, diced
1 garlic clove, minced
2 leeks, white part only, diced (1½ cups)
4 medium-size potatoes (1¼ pounds), peeled and diced
3 cups Chicken Broth (page 22), or canned
4 cups milk
2 cups grated Gruyère cheese
Salt to taste
2 tablespoons chopped fresh basil
¾ cup peeled, seeded, finely chopped, and well-drained ripe tomatoes

1. Melt butter or margarine in a large pot. Add the onion, garlic, and leeks and cook, stirring, for 5 minutes. Do not brown.
2. Add the potatoes and broth. Bring to a boil, then simmer for 20 minutes, or until the potatoes are tender and can be mashed against the side of the pot.
3. Cool slightly and pour the mixture into a blender or food processor to purée.
4. Return the puréed soup to the pot. Add the milk and heat to a simmer. Add the cheese and cook over low heat, stirring, until the cheese has melted. Taste for seasoning.
5. Serve in individual dishes with the basil and fresh tomato sprinkled on top.

MAKES ABOUT 10 CUPS, TO SERVE 6 TO 8

Chilled Potato–Beet Soup

4 large potatoes (1½ pounds)
2 cups cooked, coarsely chopped beets
4 scallions, white part only, coarsely chopped
1 teaspoon salt
½ teaspoon freshly ground pepper
3 tablespoons fresh lemon juice
1½ cups Chicken Broth (page 22), or canned
1 cup crushed ice
½ cup low-fat sour cream or yogurt
2 tablespoons minced fresh dill

1. Cook the potatoes in their skins in boiling water until tender. Drain. Dry them over low heat in the same pan. Peel and mash.
2. In the container of an electric blender, combine the potatoes, beets, scallions, salt, pepper, and lemon juice. Cover and blend at high speed.
3. With the motor running, add the chicken broth and ice. Taste for seasoning.
4. Serve chilled. Place a large dollop of sour cream or yogurt and a sprinkling of dill on top of each serving.

Serves 4

Bombay Curried Potato Soup

This deliciously smooth soup should not be served icy cold, just chilled. It's also good hot. In that case, once the half-and-half has been added, do not boil but just heat through.

2 tablespoons butter or margarine
2 medium-size onions, chopped
1 garlic clove, minced
2 teaspoons curry powder
4 large potatoes (1½ pounds), peeled and cubed
4 cups Chicken Broth (page 22), or canned
1 teaspoon celery salt
1¼ cups half-and-half
2 tablespoons minced fresh chives

1. In a large pot, melt the butter or margarine. Add the onions and garlic and cook for 2 minutes. Stir in the curry powder.
2. Add the potatoes, broth, and celery salt. Bring to a boil, reduce heat, then simmer for 20 minutes, or until the potatoes are tender. Taste for seasoning.
3. Cool slightly and blend soup in an electric blender or food processor, or push contents through a strainer.
4. Refrigerate. When ready to serve, mix in the half-and-half.
5. Sprinkle the chives on top.

SERVES 6

Potato-Carrot Soup

3 tablespoons butter or margarine
1 large onion, thinly sliced
4 medium-size potatoes (1¼ pounds), peeled and thinly sliced
3 carrots, scraped and thinly sliced
8 cups Chicken Broth (page 22), or canned
Salt and freshly ground pepper to taste
1 cup half-and-half
1 teaspoon dried dill
½ teaspoon hot pepper sauce
1 medium-size carrot, scraped and grated
1 cup low-fat sour cream or yogurt

1. In a large pot, over medium heat, melt the butter or margarine. Add the onion, potatoes, and sliced carrots, and cook, stirring, for 5 minutes.
2. Add the broth, salt, and pepper. Bring to a boil, lower heat and simmer for 20 minutes, or until the vegetables are tender.
3. Cool slightly and pour the soup into a blender or food processor to purée.
4. Stir in the half-and-half, dill, and hot pepper sauce.
5. Cook the grated carrot in boiling water for 1 minute and drain. Set aside.
6. Just before serving, stir the sour cream or yogurt into the soup and heat to a simmer. Taste for seasoning. Serve with the grated carrot sprinkled on top.

MAKES 7 1/2 CUPS, TO SERVE 4 TO 5

Potato-Cucumber Soup

7 medium-size (about 2½ pounds) potatoes, peeled and sliced
2 medium-size onions, peeled and sliced
4 tablespoons (½ stick) butter or margarine
1½ teaspoons salt
2½ cups water
2 medium-size cucumbers, peeled, seeded, and coarsely grated
2½ cups half-and-half, scalded
1½ teaspoons fresh chervil, or 1 teaspoon dried
Freshly ground pepper to taste

1. In a pot, combine the potatoes, onions, butter or margarine, salt, and water. Bring to a boil. Reduce to a simmer, cover, and cook for 30 minutes, or until the potatoes are tender.
2. Cool slightly and purée in a blender. Return the puréed mixture to the pot. Stir in the cucumbers, half-and-half, and chervil, blending well. Bring to a simmer and cook for 10 minutes. Do not boil.
3. Taste for seasoning. If soup seems too thick, add more water.

MAKES 8 CUPS, TO SERVE 4 TO 6

Parisian Summer Green Potato Soup

This tangy soup should not be served icy cold, just chilled, so the flavor comes through.

3 tablespoons butter or margarine
4 scallions, white and green parts, thinly sliced
3 medium-size leeks, white and some light green parts, thinly sliced
1 celery stalk, scraped and thinly sliced
2 cups shelled fresh peas, or one 10-ounce package frozen, thawed peas
3 large potatoes (about 1¼ pounds), peeled and cut into ¼-inch slices
4 cups Chicken Broth (page 22), or canned
Salt and freshly ground pepper to taste

1. Heat the butter or margarine in a large saucepan. Add the scallions, leeks, and celery and cook for 5 minutes.
2. Add the peas and potatoes and stir until they are well mixed with other vegetables. Pour in the broth, bring soup to a boil, reduce heat, and simmer for 20 minutes, or until the potatoes are tender. Season with salt and pepper. Cool mixture slightly.
3. Put soup through a food mill or purée in a blender or food processor.
4. Taste for seasoning. Cool and refrigerate until ready to serve.

Serves 4 to 6

Vernon Jarratt's Golden Potato Soup

Our friend Vernon Jarratt was the long-time owner of George's, one of Rome's most famous restaurants. This soup was one of his specialties.

4 tablespoons (½ stick) butter or margarine
1 medium-size onion, peeled and chopped
4 large potatoes (1½ pounds), peeled and diced
1 pound tomatoes, peeled, seeded, and put through a food mill or blender
1 quart beef broth
Salt and freshly ground pepper to taste
4 tablespoons grated Parmesan cheese
Croutons for garnish

1. In a large pot, melt 2 tablespoons butter or margarine. Add the onion and cook until slightly golden. Add the potatoes and cook, stirring, for 3 minutes. Stir in the tomatoes and cook for 10 minutes.
2. Pour in the broth. Bring the mixture to a boil, lower heat, cover, and simmer for 25 minutes. Season with salt and pepper to taste.
3. Stir in the remaining 2 tablespoons butter or margarine and half the Parmesan.
4. Ladle into hot soup bowls, sprinkle on the remaining Parmesan, and sprinkle croutons over all.

MAKES 7 CUPS, TO SERVE 4

Italian Potato Soup

8 medium-size potatoes (about 2¾ pounds), peeled and cut into 1-inch cubes
2 tablespoons butter or margarine
1 tablespoon olive oil
3 medium-size onions, finely chopped
2 carrots, scraped and cut into ¼-inch cubes
2 garlic cloves, minced
½ cup tomato purée
5 cups Chicken Broth (page 22), or canned
½ cup finely chopped celery leaves
Salt and freshly ground pepper to taste
½ cup grated Asiago or Parmesan cheese

1. Cook the potatoes in boiling, salted water until tender. Drain and mash.
2. In a large saucepan, over medium heat, heat the butter or margarine and oil and cook the onions, carrots, and garlic, stirring for 3 minutes, or until the vegetables are well coated.
3. Add the tomato purée, chicken broth, celery leaves, mashed potatoes, salt, and pepper. Simmer for 15 minutes, or until the carrots are just tender.
4. Serve with the cheese sprinkled over individual servings.

Serves 6 to 8

Soup Parmentier

This main-dish soup is a considerably heartier version of the French classic.

3 or 4 leeks
3 tablespoons butter or margarine
1 large carrot, scraped and cut into ¼-inch cubes
1 large celery stalk, scraped and cut into ¼-inch cubes
6 cups Chicken Broth (page 22), or canned
5 medium-size potatoes (1¾ pounds), peeled and cut into ½-inch cubes
1 cup chopped celery leaves
Salt and freshly ground pepper to taste
1 small unpeeled zucchini, cut into ½-inch cubes
½ cup half-and-half
2 tablespoons chopped fresh chives

1. Thoroughly wash the white and the light green part of the leeks. Slice lengthwise, then cut into ½- to 1-inch pieces.
2. Melt the butter or margarine in a large pot over medium heat. Add the leeks, carrot, and celery, and sauté for 5 minutes, stirring. Do not brown.
3. Pour in the broth and simmer, covered, for 15 minutes.
4. Add the potatoes and celery leaves. Season with salt and pepper and simmer, uncovered, for 10 minutes.
5. Add the zucchini and cook for 5 minutes, or until the potatoes and zucchini are tender but not mushy. Taste for seasoning.
6. Just before serving, stir in the half-and-half. Sprinkle the chives over each serving.

SERVES 6

La Chaudrée

This is France's contribution to the art of chowdermaking; the English word is derived from the name of this dish. Serve with hot, crusty bread.

Bouquet Garni

2 sprigs parsley
Pinch of thyme
2 bay leaves
2 whole cloves

6 large onions, cut in thick slices
1 large celery stalk, scraped and sliced
3 garlic cloves, peeled and halved
10 peppercorns, crushed
5 medium-size potatoes (1¾ pounds), peeled and cut into ½-inch-thick slices
3 tablespoons butter or margarine
3 pounds fish fillets, cod and haddock preferred, cut into 2-inch chunks
Salt and freshly ground pepper
3 cups dry white wine
3 cups water

1. To make the bouquet garni, wrap the parsley, thyme, bay leaves, and cloves in a double thickness of cheesecloth and tie into a packet using kitchen twine.
2. Layer the bottom of a large pot with the onions, celery, garlic, peppercorns, and the bouquet garni. Arrange the potato slices on top, overlapping if necessary to make one layer.
3. Dot the butter or margarine over the potatoes.
4. Arrange the fish chunks on top of the potatoes. Season with salt and pepper. Pour the wine and water over all,

cover, and bring to a boil. Reduce heat and simmer for 25 minutes, or until the potatoes are tender.

5. Taste for seasoning. Remove the bouquet garni and serve.

MAKES 4 1/2 QUARTS, TO SERVE 6

Lisbon Mashed Potato and Cabbage Soup

Water retains an amazing flavor after potatoes are boiled in it. It's the basis of this famous Portuguese soup.

5 medium-size potatoes (1¾ pounds), peeled and quartered
6 cups water
1½ teaspoons salt
½ small (1 pound) cabbage, very finely shredded
2 tablespoons olive oil
1 tablespoon butter or margarine
½ teaspoon freshly ground pepper

1. Cook the potatoes in the salted water until tender.
2. Remove potatoes from the water with a skimmer or slotted spoon, and mash them in a bowl. Reserve the potato water.
3. Return mashed potatoes to the pot of water. Stir in the cabbage, olive oil, butter or margarine, and pepper, mixing well. Bring to a boil, reduce heat, and simmer for 15 minutes, or until the cabbage is tender. Taste for seasoning.

MAKES 6 1/2 CUPS, TO SERVE 4

Potato-Spaetzle Soup

4 tablespoons (½ stick) butter or margarine
4 medium-size potatoes (1¼ pounds), peeled and cut into ½-inch cubes
1 medium-size onion, chopped
1 celery stalk, scraped and chopped
Salt and freshly ground pepper to taste
6 cups beef broth
½ cup spaetzle, cooked according to package directions
2 cups cooked diced beef, chicken, or turkey

1. In a large pot, over medium heat, melt the butter or margarine. Add the potatoes, onion, celery, salt, and pepper. Cook, stirring, for 5 minutes. Do not brown.
2. Pour in the broth and simmer for 30 minutes, or until the potatoes are tender.
3. Stir in the spaetzle and meat. Taste for seasoning.
4. Simmer until heated through.

MAKES 10½ CUPS, TO SERVE 6 TO 8

Spanish Potato–Fish Chowder

3 tablespoons olive oil
2 medium-size onions, chopped
2 garlic cloves, minced
2 small carrots, scraped and thinly sliced
3 large, ripe tomatoes, peeled, seeded, and chopped, or one 1-pound can of tomatoes, including liquid, chopped
2 cups clam broth
½ cup dry white wine (optional)
¼ cup Madeira (optional)
1 small bay leaf
Pinch of cinnamon
Pinch of saffron
Pinch of red pepper flakes
Salt and freshly ground pepper to taste
4 small potatoes (about 1 pound), peeled and cut into ¼-inch-thick slices
2 pounds salmon, red snapper, or other fish of your choice, filleted and cut into 2-inch pieces
½ teaspoon grated lemon rind
3 tablespoons chopped fresh parsley

1. Heat the oil in a large pot. Add the onions, garlic, and carrots, and cook for 5 minutes, stirring, or until the vegetables are coated with the oil and softened.
2. Add the tomatoes, clam broth, the wines, bay leaf, cinnamon, saffron, red pepper flakes, salt, and pepper. Simmer, covered, for 10 minutes.
3. Add the potatoes and simmer for another 15 minutes.
4. Add the fish. Add more water if the mixture seems thick and the fish pieces are not covered by the liquid. Simmer, uncovered, for 15 minutes, or until the potatoes are tender and the fish flakes easily with a fork.

5. Stir in the lemon rind. Remove the bay leaf. Taste for seasoning.
6. Sprinkle parsley on top of each serving.

MAKES 8 CUPS, TO SERVE 4 TO 6

Soupe au Pistou

2 quarts Chicken Broth (page 22), or canned
4 medium-size potatoes (1¼ pounds), peeled and cut into 1-inch cubes
½ pound fresh string beans, cut into 1-inch pieces
2 carrots, scraped and sliced
1 medium-size onion, chopped
2 teaspoons salt
½ teaspoon freshly ground pepper
1 small, unpeeled zucchini, cut into ¼-inch-thick slices
One 16-ounce can kidney or navy beans, drained, rinsed, and drained again

Sauce
4 garlic cloves, put through a garlic press
¼ cup tomato purée
1 tablespoon dried basil
½ cup grated Parmesan cheese
½ cup chopped fresh parsley
¼ cup olive oil

1. In a large pot, combine the chicken broth, potatoes, string beans, carrots, onion, salt, and pepper. Bring to a boil, lower the heat, and simmer, covered, for 10 minutes.
2. Add the zucchini and simmer for 10 minutes longer, or until all the vegetables are tender. Stir in the beans.

3. For the sauce, combine the garlic, tomato purée, basil, Parmesan, and parsley. Using a wire whip, gradually beat in the oil, a teaspoon at a time, until the oil emulsifies with the other ingredients to form a thick sauce.
4. Just before serving, stir the sauce into the hot soup.

MAKES 12 CUPS, TO SERVE 6 TO 8

Potato and Spinach Soup

2 tablespoons butter or margarine
1 large onion, coarsely chopped
4 medium-size potatoes (1¼ pounds), peeled and each cut into 8 pieces
2 cups Chicken Broth (page 22), or canned
One 10-ounce package fresh spinach, coarsely chopped, or one 10-ounce package frozen chopped spinach, thawed
½ teaspoon seasoned salt
½ teaspoon celery salt
Pinch of mace
Freshly ground pepper to taste
1 cup milk
1 cup half-and-half
3 tablespoons dry sherry (optional)
½ cup chopped mushrooms

1. In a large saucepan, melt the butter or margarine. Add the onion and cook for 2 minutes.
2. Add the potatoes and broth and bring to a boil. Reduce heat and simmer, covered, for 10 minutes.
3. Add the spinach, salts, mace, and pepper. Simmer for 10 minutes longer, or until the potatoes are tender.

4. Cool slightly. Put soup into a blender or food processor and purée.
5. Return puréed soup to the saucepan. Add the milk and half-and-half and heat just to a simmer. Taste for seasoning.
6. Stir in the sherry, if desired, just before serving. If the soup still seems too thick, add a small amount of hot broth.
7. Sprinkle the mushrooms on top of each serving.

Makes 8 cups, to serve 4 to 6

Vichyssoise

The classic version of this velvety smooth rich soup is traditionally served cold, but it's also good hot.

2 tablespoons butter or margarine
4 medium-size leeks, white part only, washed well and chopped
2 medium-size onions, chopped
4 medium-size potatoes (1¼ pounds), peeled and thinly sliced
4 cups Chicken Broth (page 22), or canned
¼ teaspoon nutmeg
1½ teaspoons salt
1½ cups half-and-half
2 tablespoons chopped watercress

1. In a large pot, over medium heat, melt the butter or margarine. Add the leeks and onions and cook for 5 minutes.
2. Add the potatoes and chicken broth. Cook, covered, for 15 minutes, or until the potatoes are tender.

3. Cool mixture slightly. Pour into a blender or food processor and blend for a few seconds until velvety smooth.
4. Add the nutmeg and salt and blend again for 2 or 3 seconds. Taste for seasoning. Chill soup until ready to serve.
5. Just before serving stir in the half-and-half. Garnish with the watercress and serve.

MAKES 7 CUPS, TO SERVE 5 TO 6

3

Salads

THE PICNIC, THAT GREAT AMERICAN RELAXER, IS PLANNED around people, but let's look further for the guest of honor. It must be, yes, the potato salad—the culinary masterpiece around which all the other picnic foods revolve. Hot dogs and potato salad, hamburgers and potato salad, cold sliced ham and potato salad. The potato salad makes it a perfect outdoor feast.

And that potato salad can be as varied and innovative as the imagination of the person who prepares it. The ingredients that mate well with sliced or cubed potatoes, glistening with mayonnaise or other dressings, range from sliced hard-boiled eggs and olives to lima beans, cucumbers, tuna, scallops, and mushrooms. In fact, one of the pleasures of a picnic is the anticipation of sampling a new and different potato salad.

The potato salad is also popular abroad. Most countries have their own favorites, from the hot German version to the warm Italian potato salad with black pepper, olive oil, and white wine.

All of these superb salads are even tastier if they are prepared with new potatoes. If they are unavailable, use the Round Whites or Round Reds.

Potato, Lima, and Fresh Mushroom Salad

This excellent summer repast goes well with assorted cold meats and a fresh loaf of crunchy Italian bread.

8 medium-size (about 2¾ pounds) new potatoes
1 cup baby lima beans, cooked and drained
4 scallions, white part only, chopped
4 medium-size fresh mushrooms, thinly sliced
1 tablespoon chopped fresh broadleaf parsley, or 1 teaspoon dried
1 tablespoon chopped fresh tarragon, or 1 teaspoon dried
1 tablespoon chopped fresh chervil, or 1 teaspoon dried

Dressing

¼ cup fresh lemon juice
6 tablespoons olive oil
Salt and freshly ground pepper to taste

1. Cook the potatoes in their skins in boiling water over medium heat until tender, about 25 to 30 minutes. Drain and dry over low heat in the same pan. While still warm, peel and chop the potatoes into cubes.
2. In a large bowl, combine the potatoes, lima beans, scallions, and mushrooms. Mix gently.
3. Blend together lemon juice, olive oil, salt, and pepper.

Add the dressing to the potato mixture, the amount according to your taste. Add the herbs. Toss well, but gently.
4. Serve at room temperature.

MAKES 5 CUPS, TO SERVE 4

Potato and String Bean Salad

For this salad, it's important to use small, firm new potatoes and young, tender string beans.

1½ pounds very small new potatoes
1 pound young string beans
Crisp Boston lettuce leaves
2 tablespoons minced broadleaf parsley

Dressing
½ cup olive oil
2 tablespoons dry white vermouth (optional)
2 small onions, minced
2 tablespoons minced watercress
1 tablespoon minced fresh chives
Salt and freshly ground pepper to taste

1. In boiling water over medium heat, cook the potatoes in their skins until just tender, about 15 minutes. Cool potatoes slightly. Peel and cut lengthwise into ¼-inch sticks.
2. Cook the beans in boiling, salted water for 5 minutes. Do not overcook, they should be crunchy. Chill the cooked beans in ice cold water. Drain.

3. In a large bowl, combine the potatoes and beans. In a small bowl, blend together the dressing ingredients.
4. Pour the blended dressing in stages over the potato-bean mixture, tossing gently each time. The vegetables should be well coated but not swimming in the dressing.
5. Arrange the lettuce in a salad bowl, then the potatoes and beans. Sprinkle with the parsley and serve at room temperature.

MAKES 6 1/2 CUPS, TO SERVE 4 GENEROUSLY

Danish Fisherman's Potato Salad with Piquant Mayonnaise

8 medium-size new potatoes (about 2¾ pounds)
1½ cups dry white wine (optional)
1 pound bay scallops, or sea scallops cut in quarters
½ cup water or clam broth
Piquant Mayonnaise (recipe follows)
Salt and freshly ground pepper to taste
Boston lettuce to line salad bowl
1 teaspoon capers, rinsed and drained

1. In boiling water over medium heat, cook the potatoes in their skins until tender. Drain and dry in the same pan over low heat. While the potatoes are still warm, peel and cut into ½-inch cubes. Sprinkle potatoes with ½ cup of the wine, if desired. Set aside.
2. Poach scallops in the remaining 1 cup wine, if desired, and the water or clam broth for about 6 minutes, or until

they are firm but tender. (If wine isn't used, increase other liquid proportionately.) Do not overcook. Drain and cool slightly.

3. Drain any excess wine from the potatoes. Mix the potatoes and scallops with half of the mayonnaise. Taste, then add more mayonnaise, salt, and pepper, if desired.

4. Line a salad bowl with the lettuce and arrange the salad on top. Garnish with the capers. Serve warm or chilled.

MAKES 6 CUPS, TO SERVE 6

Piquant Mayonnaise

1 cup low-fat mayonnaise
2 tablespoons fresh lemon juice
3 shallots, finely chopped
2 teaspoons capers, rinsed and drained

Combine all the ingredients and blend well.

MAKES ABOUT 1 1/4 CUPS

Barbara M. Valbona's Potato Salad

12 small new potatoes (about 1½ pounds)
1 teaspoon coarse salt
½ teaspoon freshly ground pepper
1½ tablespoons tarragon vinegar
¼ cup olive oil
½ teaspoon dry mustard
1 tablespoon chopped fresh parsley
1 teaspoon chopped fresh chives

1. Cook the potatoes in their skins in boiling water over medium heat until tender, about 15 to 20 minutes. Cool and slip off skins. Thinly slice potatoes into a large bowl.
2. In a small bowl, combine the remaining ingredients, except the parsley and chives, and add to the potatoes. Toss until the potatoes are well coated. Set mixture aside, cover, and cool.
3. Fold in the herbs. Serve at room temperature.

MAKES 4 CUPS, TO SERVE 4

Genovese Hot Potato Salad

6 medium-size potatoes (about 2 pounds)
¼ cup olive oil
3 tablespoons dry white wine
1½ teaspoons salt
½ teaspoon freshly ground pepper
1 garlic clove, minced

⅛ teaspoon dried oregano
¼ cup chopped fresh broadleaf parsley

1. In boiling water over medium heat, cook the potatoes in their skins until tender. Drain and dry in the same pan over low heat. While still warm peel the potatoes and cut into ¼-inch-thick slices. Place in a large bowl.
2. In another bowl, thoroughly blend together the oil, wine, salt, pepper, garlic, oregano, and parsley. Gently blend the dressing in with the sliced potatoes. Taste for seasoning. Serve while still warm.

MAKES 5 CUPS, TO SERVE 4

German Potato Salad

We discovered this one in Frankfurt. The mustard, sour cream, and dill are typical German touches.

8 medium-size potatoes (about 2¾ pounds)
6 scallions, white part and some green, chopped
½ cup Chicken Broth (page 22), or canned
2 tablespoons olive oil
1 tablespoon wine vinegar
½ teaspoon dry mustard
¼ teaspoon celery seed
Salt and freshly ground pepper to taste
½ cup low-fat sour cream or yogurt
2 tablespoons minced fresh dill, or 1 teaspoon dried

1. In boiling water over medium heat, cook the potatoes in their skins until tender, about 25 to 30 minutes. Drain

and dry over low heat in the same pan. While still warm, peel and cut into ¼-inch-thick slices. Set aside and keep warm.

2. In a saucepan, combine the scallions, broth, olive oil, vinegar, mustard, celery seed, salt, and pepper, and simmer for 2 minutes.

3. Cool slightly. Stir in the sour cream or yogurt, mixing well. Pour dressing over the warm potatoes and mix gently.

4. Sprinkle dill on top of salad and serve at room temperature.

MAKES 7 CUPS, TO SERVE 6

Niçoise Salad

6 medium-size new potatoes (about 2 pounds)
½ to 1 cup Vinaigrette Sauce (recipe follows)
½ pound cooked string beans, cut into 1-inch pieces
½ cup plump black Italian olives
3 scallions, white and green parts, trimmed and chopped
One 7½-ounce can solid white tuna
Crisp Boston lettuce leaves
12 anchovy fillets, drained
2 ripe tomatoes, peeled, each cut into 6 wedges, then allowed to drain for 30 minutes
2 tablespoons chopped fresh basil

1. Cook the potatoes in their skins in boiling water over medium heat until tender, about 25 to 30 minutes. Drain

and dry over low heat. Peel, and while still warm, cut into ¼-inch-thick slices.
2. Mix the warm potatoes with ¼ cup vinaigrette, and marinate in the refrigerator for 1 hour.
3. Add the green beans, olives, scallions, and tuna, plus another ¼ cup vinaigrette to the potatoes. Mix well but gently. Taste for seasoning. Add more sauce, if necessary.
4. Line a salad bowl with the lettuce leaves and spoon in the potato mixture. Arrange the anchovy fillets like the spokes of a wheel on top of the salad, with the tomato wedges in between. Sprinkle the tomatoes with basil. Refrigerate. Do not serve the salad too cold.

SERVES 6

Vinaigrette Sauce

2 tablespoons lemon juice
2 tablespoons wine vinegar
¾ cup olive oil
1 garlic clove, minced
¼ teaspoon Dijon mustard
½ teaspoon sugar
¾ teaspoon salt
½ teaspoon freshly ground pepper

Combine all ingredients and mix well.

MAKES ABOUT 1 CUP

Pasquale's Potato Salad

This was our father's and father-in-law's specialty. It is a simple salad but has surprising authority. Pasquale liked to serve it with a cold roast veal or lamb that was sprinkled with lemon juice.

Mix the potatoes with the dressing while they are still warm, and make sure to use freshly ground pepper from a pepper mill.

6 medium-size new potatoes (about 2 pounds)
1 teaspoon of salt
Freshly ground pepper to taste
5 tablespoons extra-virgin olive oil
Plump black Italian olives, for garnish

1. Cook the potatoes in their skins in boiling water over medium heat until tender, about 25 to 30 minutes. Drain and dry over low heat in the same pan. While still warm, peel and cube the potatoes.
2. In a bowl, combine the warm potatoes, salt, and a liberal grinding of fresh black pepper.
3. Add the olive oil, tossing well but gently so the potato cubes remain intact. Taste for seasoning.
4. Garnish with the olives and serve at room temperature.

Makes 2 cups, to serve 4

Potato–Tuna Salad

This is a light but delicious meal in itself. Great for a hot day when the kitchen is off limits.

1 tablespoon fresh lemon juice
1 garlic clove, crushed
¾ cup low-fat mayonnaise
6 medium-size new potatoes (about 2 pounds)
One 6½-ounce can solid white tuna, drained and broken into small, bite-size pieces
2 celery stalks, scraped and diced
Salt and freshly ground pepper to taste
4 hard-boiled eggs, halved crosswise

1. In a small bowl, blend together the lemon juice, crushed garlic, and mayonnaise to make garlic mayonnaise. Set aside.
2. Cook the potatoes in their skins in boiling water over medium heat until tender, about 30 minutes. Drain and dry over low heat in the same pan. While still warm, peel and cube the potatoes.
3. Place the potatoes, tuna, and celery in a large bowl. Toss gently.
4. Add the garlic mayonnaise, salt, and pepper to taste. Toss gently, but blend well.
5. Chill and serve garnished with the eggs.

SERVES 4

Potato Salad Turkish Style

We serve this satisfying dish with cold chicken broiled with lemon juice.

6 medium-size new potatoes (about 2 pounds)
¼ cup wine vinegar with garlic

Dressing

3 tablespoons lemon juice
½ cup olive oil
½ teaspoon dry mustard
½ teaspoon ground cumin
2 tablespoons chopped broadleaf parsley
2 tablespoons chopped fresh mint leaves
Salt and freshly ground pepper to taste

12 plump black Italian olives
4 large radishes, sliced
2 scallions, white part and some green, coarsely chopped

1. Cook the potatoes in their skins in boiling water over medium heat until tender, about 25 to 30 minutes. Drain and dry over low heat in the same pan. While still warm, peel and cube potatoes.
2. Place the potatoes in a bowl with the vinegar and toss well but gently. Marinate potatoes for 30 minutes, then pour off any excess vinegar. Set aside.
3. For the dressing, blend together the lemon juice, olive oil, mustard, cumin, parsley, mint, salt, and pepper. Add half the dressing and the olives to the potatoes. Mix well but carefully. Taste for seasoning. Add more dressing, if desired.
4. Garnish with radishes and sprinkle the scallions on top. Serve at room temperature.

SERVES 6

4

Potato Specialties

THESE ARE, INDEED, VERY SPECIAL AND UNIQUE RECIPES, RANGing from poultry stuffing to dumplings, muffins, and croquettes.

This chapter is the one to turn to when you need to add a new dimension to your dining. For example, you can add taste, intrigue, and mystery by blending sauerkraut with creamy mashed potatoes, as the Dutch do, or by mixing potatoes with applesauce, as the Germans like to offer with pork. Or transform leftover mashed potatoes into plump, tasty dumplings.

Baked potato skins cut into 1-inch strips make unique hors d'oeuvres. Arrange the strips on a cookie sheet, then brush with butter or margarine, and sprinkle with salt, pepper, grated Parmesan cheese, or mixed herbs. Bake to crisp goodness at 475°F in just about 8 minutes.

The point to be made: The potato is indeed a very special food. Used with imagination, it can enhance and enliven your everyday dining.

Potato–Apple Stuffing

This special stuffing goes well with any bird but is especially good with duck or a large holiday goose. You can make a superb sauce right in the roasting pan: Drain off most of the fat, add 2 tablespoons wine vinegar, liquid from cooked onions, a little half-and-half, and a jigger of orange liqueur to the pan. Stir and heat through.

It's recommended that you stuff the bird immediately before putting it into the oven.

3 medium-size potatoes (1 pound)
Grated rind of 1 small orange
1 large unpeeled apple, finely chopped
¼ cup freshly squeezed orange juice
2 medium-size onions, minced
1½ teaspoons salt
½ teaspoon freshly ground pepper

1. Cook the potatoes in their skins in boiling water over medium heat until tender. Drain. Dry them over low heat in the same pan. Peel and mash.
2. In a bowl, blend the orange rind, apple, and potatoes.
3. In a saucepan, bring the orange juice to a boil. Reduce to a simmer and cook the onions in the juice for 10 minutes, or until soft.
4. Drain the onions. Save the liquid for a sauce (see above).
5. Whip the onions, salt, and pepper into the potato mixture. Taste for seasoning.

MAKES APPROXIMATELY
3 CUPS STUFFING, ENOUGH
FOR A 10- TO 12-POUND BIRD

Potato-Carrot Muffins

6 cups grated raw potatoes (about 3 pounds), well drained and squeezed dry in a kitchen towel
3 egg yolks, beaten
½ cup grated raw carrots
5 tablespoons melted butter or margarine
1½ teaspoons salt
1 teaspoon baking powder
1 cup sifted all-purpose flour
3 egg whites, stiffly beaten

1. In a bowl, combine and beat with a wire whisk the potatoes, egg yolks, carrots, butter or margarine, salt, baking powder, and flour. Gently fold in the egg whites.
2 Lightly butter a muffin tin and fill each cup two-thirds full with the mixture.
3. Bake in a preheated 425°F oven for 18 minutes, or until a toothpick inserted into a muffin comes out clean.

MAKES ABOUT 24 MUFFINS

Charlie's Corn 'Taters

This was a favorite dish of a farmer-neighbor of ours when we lived on our farm "Bluff's End" in Roxbury, Connecticut. It was made only when the corn could be picked fresh from the fields. Charlie Squires served these with his farm-raised tender pork chops and apple cider (a little on the hard side). Ah, memories!

4 medium-size potatoes (about 1¼ pounds), peeled and grated (about 2 cups)
3 young, tender ears fresh corn, husked and kernels cut from the cob (about 2 cups)
5 tablespoons all-purpose flour
2 eggs, beaten
3 tablespoons milk
1½ teaspoons salt
½ teaspoon freshly ground pepper
Vegetable oil for frying

1. Place grated potatoes in cold water to prevent browning. Drain the potatoes and place in a cloth, squeezing them very dry. In a bowl, blend together the potatoes, corn, flour, eggs, milk, salt, and pepper.
2. In a frying pan, heat ½ inch of oil until it sizzles. Scoop the batter out of the bowl with a tablespoon and cook 4 'taters at a time in the oil, until golden brown on all sides.
3. Drain on paper towels.

MAKES EIGHTEEN 3-INCH PATTIES, TO SERVE 4

Potato-Cheese Puff

5 medium-size potatoes (about 1¾ pounds)
4 tablespoons (½ stick) butter or margarine, softened
2 egg yolks
¾ cup grated sharp Cheddar cheese
Salt and freshly ground pepper to taste
2 egg whites, stiffly beaten

1. Cook the potatoes in their skins in boiling water over medium heat until tender, about 25 to 30 minutes. Drain

and dry over low heat in the same pan. Remove skins and put potatoes through a potato ricer.
2. In a bowl, combine the potatoes, butter or margarine, egg yolks, cheese, salt, and pepper. Gently fold in the egg whites.
3. Spoon batter into a buttered 1½-quart casserole. Bake in a preheated 400°F oven for 25 minutes, or until the potatoes are puffed and golden.

SERVES 4 TO 6

Potato Croquettes with Guacamole Sauce

5 medium-size potatoes (1¾ pounds)
1 cup water
3 tablespoons cornmeal
2 tablespoons butter or margarine, softened
½ cup grated sharp Cheddar cheese
Salt and freshly ground pepper to taste
1 tablespoon vegetable oil
½ stick (¼ cup) butter or margarine
2 cups chopped, cooked chicken or pork (about ½ pound)
½ teaspoon ground cumin
½ teaspoon salt
Guacamole Sauce (recipe follows)

1. Cook the potatoes in their skins in boiling water over medium heat until tender, about 25 to 30 minutes. Drain and dry over low heat in the same pan. Remove skins and mash. Keep warm.
2. Heat water, add cornmeal, and mix well. Bring to a boil,

then simmer 1 minute, stirring constantly with a wire whisk to prevent lumps.
3. Combine the mashed potatoes, the hot cornmeal, the soft butter or margarine, cheese, salt, and pepper. Mix well until batter is smooth. Shape ¼-cup portions into flat croquettes or patties.
4. Heat the oil and the ½ stick butter or margarine in a large frying pan and brown the croquettes. Drain on paper towels. Add more butter or margarine and oil, if needed, and fry the remaining croquettes.
5. Season meat with cumin and salt and mix with ½ cup of Guacamole Sauce.
6. Spoon equal amounts of the chopped meat on the croquettes and top with the remaining sauce.

Makes 15 croquettes, to serve 4 to 6

Guacamole Sauce

2 ripe avocados
3 tablespoons fresh lime juice
2 scallions, white part and some green, minced
1 large ripe tomato, peeled, seeded, and finely chopped
1 hot green chili, minced, or a good pinch of red pepper flakes
1 tablespoon chopped fresh coriander, or ½ teaspoon ground
Salt to taste
3 slices crisply cooked bacon, drained on paper towels and crumbled (optional)

1. Peel, pit, and mash the avocados.
2. Add the remaining ingredients, except the bacon, and blend until smooth.
3. Stir in the bacon just before serving.

MAKES APPROXIMATELY 1 1/2 CUPS

Potato-Fish Balls with Cucumber Sauce

2 cups finely chopped cooked fish (about ¾ pound)
4 cups finely chopped cooked potatoes (about 1½ pounds)
2 eggs, beaten
2 tablespoons half-and-half or milk
1 tablespoon fresh minced dill, or 1 teaspoon dried
1 teaspoon salt
½ teaspoon freshly ground pepper
Vegetable oil for frying
Cucumber Sauce (recipe follows)

1. In a bowl, combine all the ingredients except the oil. Shape into balls about 2 inches in diameter, then roll between your palms, making the balls slightly longer than wide.
2. Over medium heat, cook the fish balls in hot oil to cover until golden. Drain on paper towels.
3. Serve with Cucumber Sauce.

MAKES ABOUT 16 FISH BALLS, TO SERVE 4 TO 6

Cucumber Sauce

1 medium-size cucumber
3 tablespoons butter or margarine
3 tablespoons all-purpose flour
1 cup milk
1 cup half-and-half
Salt and freshly ground pepper to taste

1. Peel the cucumber and cut into quarters lengthwise. Cut out the seeds and discard. Coarsely chop the cucumber and place in a sieve to drain.
2. In a frying pan over medium heat, melt the butter or margarine. Stir in the flour and cook, stirring constantly, until you have a smooth paste. Gradually stir in the milk, then the half-and-half, and cook, stirring, until you have a medium-thick, smooth sauce. Season with salt and pepper.
3. Mix in the cucumber. Serve sauce with the fish balls.

Makes about 2 cups

French Potato Pie

This is a spectacular accompaniment to a perfectly cooked pink fillet of beef.

7 medium-size potatoes (about 2¼ pounds)
Pastry for a double-crust 10-inch pie, preferably homemade

2 medium-size onions, chopped
4 garlic cloves, minced
1½ teaspoons salt
½ teaspoon freshly ground pepper
¼ teaspoon mace
2 tablespoons butter or margarine
⅓ cup half-and-half or milk
1 egg, lightly beaten
1 teaspoon chopped fresh broadleaf parsley
1 teaspoon chopped fresh chives

1. Peel potatoes and cut into paper-thin slices. Cook slices in boiling water to cover for 15 minutes. Drain and set aside.
2 Divide the pastry into two parts, one slightly larger than the other. Roll out the larger part and line a 10-inch pie plate with it.
3. Arrange a layer of the precooked potato slices on the pastry; sprinkle with some of the onions, garlic, salt, pepper, and mace. Dot with butter or margarine. Repeat layers until all the potatoes, onions, and garlic are used. Pour half of the half-and-half or milk over the potatoes.
4. Roll out the remaining pastry and cover the pie. With wet fingers, seal the edges and then cut a slit in the center of the pastry.
5. Blend the egg with the remaining half-and-half or milk and lightly brush the top of the pie with the mixture. Reserve the remainder.
6. Bake pie in a preheated 400°F oven for 25 minutes, or until the crust is barely golden brown.
7. Blend the parsley and chives with the remaining egg-and-half-and-half mixture. Pour the mixture into the pie using a small funnel inserted into the center slit. Bake for another 10 minutes.

SERVES 6

George's Fennel Potato Pudding

3 eggs, beaten
1 teaspoon baking powder
¼ cup potato starch (available in supermarkets)
4 tablespoons (½ stick) butter or margarine, melted
6 medium-size baking potatoes (about 2 pounds), peeled, grated, and squeezed dry in a kitchen towel
1 medium-size onion, grated
1½ teaspoons salt
½ teaspoon freshly ground pepper
1 teaspoon crushed fennel seeds

1. In a bowl, combine the eggs, baking powder, potato starch, and half the butter or margarine.
2. Add the potatoes, blending well. Stir in the onion, salt, pepper, and fennel seeds.
3. Lightly butter a baking dish, and spoon in the potato mixture. Smooth the top without pressing down too much. Dot with the remaining butter or margarine.
4. Bake, covered, in a preheated 350°F oven for 40 minutes. Uncover and bake for another 15 minutes at 400°F, or until the potatoes are cooked through and the top is golden.

SERVES 4 TO 6

German Mashed Potatoes with Applesauce

In this slightly sweet-sour dish, the potatoes should be well dried as other liquids are added later. Do not add any liquid until all the water in the pan has evaporated.

5 medium-size potatoes (1¾ pounds)
About ½ cup hot milk
2 tablespoons butter or margarine, softened
1 teaspoon salt
⅛ teaspoon nutmeg
¼ cup warm applesauce
1 tablespoon white vinegar
2 teaspoons sugar

1. Cook the potatoes in their skins in boiling water, over medium heat until tender, about 25 to 30 minutes. Drain and dry potatoes over low heat in the same pan. Peel the potatoes and put through a ricer or food mill. Place the potatoes in a pan over low heat to dry them thoroughly. Shake and stir frequently.
2. In a bowl, whip together the potatoes, milk, butter or margarine, salt, and nutmeg. Beat in the applesauce, vinegar, and sugar. Heat thoroughly but carefully.

SERVES 4

Potato and Ham Croquettes

This makes a superb breakfast dish with a poached or fried egg on top.

3 medium-size potatoes (about 1 pound)
4 tablespoons (½ stick) butter or margarine
3 scallions, white part only, minced
1½ cups minced cooked ham (6 ounces)
¼ teaspoon dry mustard
Freshly ground pepper to taste
Salt to taste
Flour for dredging, about 1 to 2 tablespoons
1 tablespoon olive oil

1. Cook the potatoes in their skins in boiling water over medium heat until tender, about 25 minutes. Drain, and dry them over low heat in the same pan. Peel and mash.
2. In a frying pan, melt 1 tablespoon butter or margarine. Over medium heat, cook the scallions for 1 minute.
3. In a bowl, combine the mashed potatoes, ham, scallions, mustard, and pepper. Taste for seasoning. Add salt, if necessary (the ham may have supplied enough). Form into 3-by-2-by-½-inch croquettes. Dredge with flour.
4. Heat the remaining 3 tablespoons butter or margarine with the oil and brown croquettes on both sides. Add more oil, if needed.

Makes 8 croquettes, to serve 4

Potato Knishes

Chicken fat is traditional in this classic Jewish dish, but substitute butter or margarine, if you prefer.

¼ cup rendered chicken fat
3 shallots, minced
9 medium-size mushrooms, finely chopped (about 1 cup)
2 cups freshly riced cooked potatoes (about 1 pound), cooled
½ cup potato or all-purpose flour
1 egg, beaten
1 teaspoon salt
½ teaspoon freshly ground pepper

1. In a saucepan, over medium heat, melt the fat or butter or margarine and cook the shallots for 3 minutes, or until soft. Do not brown. Add the mushrooms and cook over high heat, stirring, until most of the moisture cooks off. Set aside.
2. In a bowl, combine the potatoes, flour, egg, salt, and pepper. Mix into a smooth dough.
3. Divide dough into 12 parts, about 2 tablespoons and 2 inches in diameter each. Flatten each into a 4-inch circle. Place a heaping teaspoon of the mushroom mixture in the center of each circle, then pull the dough around the mushrooms, completely encasing them to form the knish.
4. Lightly butter a baking sheet. Arrange the knishes on the sheet, making sure they do not touch. Bake in a preheated 375°F oven for 25 minutes, or until golden.

MAKES ABOUT 12 KNISHES

Mashed Potato Dumplings

Add these dumplings to any type of stew or hearty soup to make a delicious, satisfying main dish.

1½ cups all-purpose flour
1 teaspoon salt
2 teaspoons baking powder
1 tablespoon minced fresh parsley
½ cup leftover mashed potatoes
3 tablespoons vegetable shortening
1 egg
3 tablespoons milk

1. In a bowl, combine the flour, salt, baking powder, and parsley.
2. Add the potatoes and shortening. Using a pastry blender, work the flour mixture until it resembles coarse meal.
3. In a small bowl, combine the egg and milk and beat lightly. Stir the egg-milk mixture into the flour, making a soft dough. Divide dough into 12 balls.
4. Add the dumplings to a simmering stew or soup. Simmer, uncovered, for 5 minutes, and then cover and cook for 15 minutes longer, until dumplings float to the top, if depth of liquid allows.

Serves 4 to 6

Potatoes Moussaka

This Greek specialty is usually prepared with ground lamb. We prefer our meatless version, served as an accompaniment to juicy, medium-rare loin lamb chops.

4 tablespoons olive oil
6 large potatoes (about 3 pounds), peeled and cut into ¼-inch-thick slices
2 garlic cloves, minced
2 medium-size onions, chopped
5 large, ripe tomatoes, peeled, seeded, and chopped
3 tablespoons fresh lemon juice
1½ teaspoons salt
½ teaspoon freshly ground pepper
⅓ cup pignolias (pine nuts)
1 tablespoon chopped fresh mint
1½ cups finely crumbled feta cheese (about 5 ounces)

1. In a deep saucepan, heat 2 tablespoons of the oil. Quickly brown the potato slices, one layer at a time on both sides, adding more oil as needed. Drain potatoes on paper towels.
2. In the same pan, over medium heat, cook the garlic and onion until soft, adding more oil if necessary. Do not brown. Add the tomatoes, lemon juice, salt, pepper, pignolias, and mint. Blend. Cover and simmer over low heat for 8 minutes. Stir occasionally.
3. Stir half of the cheese into the mixture and cook, uncovered, for 10 minutes, stirring until the sauce is smooth and thick. Taste for seasoning.
4. Butter a large baking dish or casserole and arrange a layer of the potato slices on the bottom. Spoon some of the sauce over the potatoes. Repeat the layers, ending with a layer of sauce on top. Sprinkle with the remaining cheese.

5. Bake, covered, in a preheated 375°F oven for 20 minutes. Uncover and bake for 10 more minutes, or until the potatoes are tender.

Serves 6

Neapolitan Pissaladière

This robust dish gives a new dimension to pizza.

4 medium-size, ripe but firm, peeled tomatoes
Potato Piecrust (page 72) dough
Olive oil
1 cup cubed Fontina cheese (about 6 ounces)
½ teaspoon dried oregano
½ teaspoon dried basil
Salt and freshly ground pepper to taste
½ cup grated Asiago or Parmesan cheese
12 pitted black olives, halved lengthwise
One 2-ounce can anchovy fillets

1. Slice the tomatoes and drain in a large strainer for up to 1 hour.
2. Meanwhile, roll the pastry into a 12-inch circle or into the shape of the pan you intend to use (it should be very shallow). Lightly oil the pan. Place the pastry in it and bake in a preheated 350°F oven for 10 minutes, or until the edges are golden. (If the pastry puffs during the cooking, prick it in several places with a fork.) Brush the top with olive oil.
3. Arrange the tomato slices on the pastry. Sprinkle on the Fontina, oregano, basil, salt, and pepper. Lightly drizzle with olive oil. Sprinkle on the grated cheese.

4. Arrange the olives and anchovies on top and bake in a preheated 400°F oven for 15 minutes, or until the cheese is bubbling and golden.

SERVES 6

New Potatoes Poached in Herbs

Here is a specialty from our mentor, the great French chef Antoine Gilly. He loves new potatoes, fresh from the ground. Use small, but not tiny, new potatoes, large enough to allow 4 per serving.

Bouquet Garni

1 celery stalk, quartered
1 sprig broadleaf parsley
1 bay leaf
½ teaspoon dried oregano
½ teaspoon dried marjoram
½ teaspoon dried thyme

3 garlic cloves, crushed
1 medium-size yellow onion, halved
2 teaspoons salt
16 small new potatoes (about 1¾ pounds), unpeeled
2 tablespoons extra virgin olive oil
Freshly ground black pepper to taste

1. To make the bouquet garni, wrap the herbs in a double thickness of cheesecloth and tie into a packet using kitchen twine.
2. Place the garlic, onion, salt, and bouquet garni in a large pot. Cover with water and bring to a boil over medium-

high heat. Cover the pot, lower heat, and simmer 30 minutes.
3. Add the potatoes to the pot and simmer for 20 minutes, or until the potatoes are tender. Drain well. Discard the bouquet garni, garlic, and onion. Dry the potatoes in the same pot over low heat.
4. In a small pot, warm the olive oil and add to the potatoes. Roll the potatoes in the oil to coat lightly. Grind some fresh pepper over them. Serve very hot.

Serves 4

Potato Piecrust

This is a great way to use leftover mashed potatoes. Use it for a meat or vegetable pie or to make pizza.

1½ cups all-purpose flour
1 teaspoon salt
½ teaspoon sugar
½ cup cold, unseasoned mashed potatoes
¼ cup (½ stick) butter or margarine
¼ cup vegetable shortening
1 to 2 tablespoons water

1. Combine the flour, salt, and sugar in a bowl. Add the mashed potatoes and mix well. Cut in the butter or margarine and shortening with a pastry cutter until rice-size particles are formed. Add the water and mix well with a fork.
2. Lightly knead the mixture into a ball. Wrap dough in plastic wrap and chill for 1 hour.

3. Roll out the dough between sheets of lightly floured wax paper into the desired thickness and size.

TWO 8-INCH PIECRUSTS,
ONE 8-BY-12-INCH PIECRUST TOP,
OR ONE 12-INCH PIZZA CRUST

Stuffed Clams

12 large clams, scrubbed and steamed
2 tablespoons butter or margarine
½ cup scraped and minced celery
2 tablespoons chopped shallots
Pinch of dried thyme
1½ cups mashed potatoes
1 egg, beaten
½ teaspoon Worcestershire sauce
2 tablespoons half-and-half or milk
Salt and freshly ground pepper to taste
Melted butter or margarine
Paprika

1. Remove the clams from their shells, reserving the liquid and the shells. Chop the clams and set aside.
2. In a large frying pan, over medium heat, melt the butter or margarine. Add the celery and shallots and cook for about 1 minute. Remove pan from heat.
3. Stir in the thyme, potatoes, chopped clams, egg, Worcestershire, half-and-half or milk, salt, pepper, and enough of the clam liquid to slightly moisten the mixture. Taste for seasoning.
4. Lightly butter 12 of the largest shells and evenly spoon

in the stuffing. Sprinkle each one with the melted butter or margarine and paprika.

5. Place stuffed shells on a baking sheet and bake in a preheated 375°F oven for 15 or 20 minutes, or until tops are golden.

Makes enough stuffing for 12 large clam shells

5

Substantial Provider—Main Dish Recipes

MAKE NO MISTAKE, THE POTATO IS HAUTE CUISINE. THE potato was the favorite vegetable of Madame de Pompadour, mistress of France's King Louis XV. In an attempt to prove she could match the talents of the most famous male chef of the day, she concocted *Potatoes Pompadour,* an elegant crown of mashed potatoes filled with rich creamed fish. She succeeded. Madame de Pompadour's name was added to the list of elegant French potato dishes.

The lure of the potato lies not only in its versatility and nutritive content, but in its almost perfect texture and taste, which pair perfectly with other ingredients to provide a complete main-dish meal. Combine the potato with bits of leftover beef, chicken, or any other cooked meat in a main-dish casserole to create your own "Pompadour." Concoct great hashes using canned or leftover meats and potatoes; make elegant pies with mashed potatoes and leftover or freshly cooked lamb or beef; fill puffy, magnificent potato soufflés with sauced meat; stuff omelets with potatoes; layer sliced potatoes with ham and cream to make a delicious substantial scalloped dish.

Without the potato, of course, all of these dishes lose their credibility. Ever try making hash without a potato? How about a potatoless scalloped dish? Or imagine a shepherd's pie without the mashed potatoes.

The recipes in this chapter prove that easy, delicious, inexpensive main dish entrées are always an option, thanks to the potato.

Potatoes Abruzzese

We discovered this hearty dish in the Abruzzi region, home of some of Italy's best cooks.

You'll need a large frying pan for this dish—and a large appetite. Serve with warm, crusty Italian bread.

4 sweet Italian low-fat turkey sausages
4 hot Italian low-fat turkey sausages
3 to 5 tablespoons olive oil
2 medium-size green peppers, cored and cut into ¼-inch-thick slices
4 medium-size potatoes (1½ pounds), peeled and cut into ¼-inch-thick slices
3 medium-size yellow onions, thinly sliced

1. Pierce the sausages in several places so the casings won't burst while cooking.
2. In a large frying pan, heat the 3 tablespoons olive oil. Add the sausages and cook until evenly browned.
3. If the sausages have absorbed all the oil, add 2 more tablespoons. Add the peppers and potatoes to the sausages in the pan. Cover and cook over medium heat for 15 minutes, or until the peppers and potatoes are almost tender.

4. Add the onions to the pan. Cover and cook for 15 minutes, or until the onions are soft.

SERVES 4

Potatoes Baked with Haddock

5 medium-size Idaho potatoes (about 1¾ pounds), peeled and cut into ⅛-inch-thick slices
2 garlic cloves, finely chopped
¼ cup chopped fresh broadleaf parsley
1 teaspoon dried dill
¼ cup olive oil
Salt and freshly ground pepper to taste
4 large haddock steaks
¼ cup dry bread crumbs

1. In a bowl, combine the potatoes with half the chopped garlic, parsley, dill, and olive oil. Add salt and pepper and blend well.
2. Evenly line the bottom of a casserole (large enough to hold the four fish steaks in one neat layer) with the potato slices. Bake, uncovered, in a preheated 450°F oven for 15 minutes, or until the potatoes are almost tender. Remove from the oven.
3. Place the haddock steaks on top of the potatoes. In the bowl used for the potatoes, combine the remaining garlic, parsley, dill, and oil. Pour over the fish. Lightly season with salt and pepper and sprinkle with the bread crumbs. Bake, uncovered, in a 400°F oven for 12 minutes.
4. Baste the potatoes and fish well with the oil mixture in

the casserole and bake another 6 minutes, or until the fish flakes easily with a fork.

Serves 4

Potatoes Baked with Lean Steak

Believe it or not, this is a low-cost, economical meal. When you buy a piece of bottom round for pot roast, cut off 4 steaks about ½ inch thick. Remove all of the fat. Pound steaks well with a mallet, or with the edge of a plate. Serve with warm, crusty bread.

1 cup flour
Salt and freshly ground pepper to taste
Four ½-inch-thick slices bottom round (about 6 ounces each), well pounded
1 tablespoon butter or margarine
1 tablespoon olive oil
2 cups beef broth
4 medium-size potatoes (about 1¼ pounds), peeled and cut into ¼-inch-thick slices
3 medium-size onions, thinly sliced

1. Mix flour, 1 teaspoon salt, and ½ teaspoon pepper together on a sheet of wax paper. Dredge the steaks evenly in the flour mixture.
2. In a frying pan, heat the butter or margarine and oil. Over medium heat, brown the steaks on both sides. Remove steaks from pan and set aside.
3. Pour the beef broth into the frying pan and stir, scraping the bottom of the pan to loosen the browned particles. Simmer for 5 minutes.

4. In a shallow casserole, arrange the potatoes in one layer, overlapping. Sprinkle lightly with salt and pepper and cover with a layer of onions. Place the browned steaks on the onions and pour the beef broth over all. Cover and bake in a preheated 375°F oven for 45 minutes, or until potatoes and steaks are tender.
5. Spoon the pan juices over the steaks and potatoes and serve.

SERVES 4

Potato and Beef Soufflé

If eggs are a problem for you, try using a cholesterol-free egg substitute instead of the yolks.

6 medium-size potatoes (about 2 pounds)
4 tablespoons (½ stick) butter or margarine, softened
½ cup warm milk
Salt and freshly ground pepper to taste
¼ teaspoon nutmeg
½ cup grated Gruyère cheese
5 egg yolks, well beaten
5 egg whites, stiffly beaten
4 cups (about 1 pound) cubed cooked roast beef
Brown Sauce (recipe follows)

1. Cook the potatoes in their skins in boiling water over medium heat until tender. Drain and dry over low heat in the same pan. Peel the potatoes and put through a potato ricer or food mill into a large bowl.
2. Combine the potatoes with the butter or margarine, milk, salt, pepper, nutmeg, and cheese. Beat well with an

electric beater. When mixture is slightly cooled, beat in the egg yolks, or egg substitute, blending well. Fold in the egg whites.

3. Place one third of the potato mixture in the bottom of a buttered deep 9-inch baking dish. Leaving aside enough of the potatoes to cover the top, make a ½-inch-thick lining for the sides of the dish with the potatoes.

4. Mix the beef cubes with some of the brown sauce, until the pieces are well coated. Spoon the beef cubes over the layer of potatoes. Cover with an even layer of the remaining potatoes. Bake, uncovered, in a preheated 375°F oven for 1 hour, or until mixture is set and the top is golden.

5. Serve with the remaining brown sauce.

SERVES 6

Brown Sauce

3 tablespoons butter or margarine
1 small onion, finely chopped
1 small garlic clove, minced
Pinch of thyme
Salt and freshly ground pepper to taste
3 tablespoons flour
2½ cups warm beef broth
¼ cup tomato purée

1. In a saucepan, over medium heat, melt the butter or margarine. Cook the onion and garlic until the onion is soft. Do not brown.

2. Add the thyme, salt, and pepper. Stir in the flour, blending well.

3. Blend together the beef broth and tomato purée, then

stir into the saucepan, a small amount at a time, blending into a smooth, medium-thick sauce. Taste for seasoning.

MAKES ABOUT 2 CUPS

Potato-Broccoli Purée with Scrambled Eggs

Use cholesterol-free egg substitute in this dish, if you wish.

6 medium-size potatoes (2 pounds)
9 large eggs
2 tablespoons butter or margarine
Salt and freshly ground pepper to taste
One 10-ounce package frozen chopped broccoli
1 tablespoon chopped fresh broadleaf parsley
Watercress

1. Cook potatoes in their skins in boiling water over medium heat until tender. Drain. Dry them over low heat in the same pan. Peel and mash. Keep hot.
2. Season the eggs with salt and pepper, then scramble them in the butter or margarine. Keep warm.
3. Cook the broccoli according to package directions. Drain well and purée in a blender.
4. In a large bowl, combine the mashed potatoes, puréed broccoli, and the parsley. Blend well. Season with salt and pepper to taste.
5. Place the puréed mixture on a large warm serving platter and top with the scrambled eggs.
6. Garnish with the watercress.

SERVES 6

Potato-Cabbage Casserole, Hungarian Style

6 medium-size potatoes (about 2 pounds)
1 medium-size savoy cabbage, trimmed, shredded, and center core removed
Salt
1 tablespoon cider vinegar
4 slices lean boiled ham, coarsely chopped
Freshly ground pepper to taste
¾ cup half-and-half or low-fat milk
¼ cup bread crumbs
2 tablespoons butter or margarine

1. Cook the potatoes in their skins in boiling water over medium heat until almost tender. Drain and dry over low heat in the same pan. Peel and cut potatoes into slices slightly more than ¼ inch thick. Set aside.
2. Cook the cabbage in a small amount of simmering, salted water with the vinegar, covered, until crisp-tender. Do not overcook. Drain.
3. Butter a deep baking dish. Alternate layers of potatoes and cabbage, sprinkling each layer with the ham, pepper, and if necessary, salt. (The ham provides salt as well.) The last layer should be cabbage.
4. Pour the half-and-half or milk over the top layer. Sprinkle on the bread crumbs and dot with butter or margarine. Bake in a preheated 375°F oven for 30 minutes, or until heated through and the top golden.

SERVES 4

Chips and Fish

In any other cookbook, the fish would come first. Not here!

For best results, don't cook too many at one time and don't add salt. Let the guest at the table do that.

Vegetable oil
5 medium-size Idahoes (about 1¾ pounds), peeled and cut into ⅜-by-⅜-inch strips

Batter for Fish

1 egg yolk
2 tablespoons butter or margarine, melted
1 cup flour
⅔ cup buttermilk
½ teaspoon salt
1 egg white, stiffly beaten

2 pounds boned cod or haddock, cut into 2-by-4-inch pieces

1. Heat 4 inches oil in a deep-fryer to 375°F.
2. Dry the potatoes well with a kitchen towel or paper towels—they must be very dry to cook properly. Cook potatoes 4 to 7 minutes. Don't overcook; the potatoes should be golden and crisp. Try a few first as a test, then proceed with the rest.
3. Drain the cooked potatoes on paper towels and keep warm in a 250°F oven while the rest are cooking. (Fry the fish in the same oil, but discard the oil afterward.)
4. In a large bowl, using a wire whisk, whip together the egg yolk, butter or margarine, flour, buttermilk, and salt into a smooth batter. Fold in the egg white.

5. Dry fish pieces thoroughly; fish must be very dry to absorb batter. Drop the pieces of fish, a few at a time, into the batter, coating them well. Reheat the oil to 375°F.
6. Using a slotted spoon, lower the fish (no more than 3 pieces at a time) into the oil. Cook for 4 minutes. Fish should be golden on the outside but still moist inside and should flake easily when cut with a fork.
7. Drain the fish on paper towels and place in the warm oven with the chips. When ready to serve, arrange the chips and fish on a large hot platter and serve.

SERVES 4

Colcannon

The Irish use leftover cooked potatoes and cabbage to make this unusual meal. We like this dish so much that we prepare fresh ingredients for it and don't wait for leftovers.

The addition of eggs is optional; they are often omitted from the classic Irish version.

Colcannon is sometimes served as one large cake; sometimes leftover cold lamb is added. Often it is sprinkled with cheese and browned in the oven.

5 medium-size potatoes (1¾ pounds)
4 tablespoons (½ stick) butter or margarine
4 medium-size onions, chopped
2 cups cooked, chopped cabbage
Salt and freshly ground pepper to taste
1 tablespoon olive oil
4 to 6 eggs, poached (optional)

1. Cook the potatoes in their skins in boiling water over medium heat until tender. Drain. Dry them over low heat in the same pan. Peel and mash.
2. Melt 2 tablespoons butter or margarine in a saucepan, over medium heat. Add the onions and cook until soft. Do not brown.
3. In a large bowl, combine the onions, cabbage, mashed potatoes, salt, and pepper. Shape mixture into 4 to 6 thick patties.
4. In a frying pan, heat the remaining 2 tablespoons of butter or margarine and the olive oil. Brown the patties evenly in the butter and oil. Top with poached eggs, if desired. Serve on warm plates.

SERVES 4 TO 6

Curried Potatoes with Scallions and Eggs

8 large eggs, or cholesterol-free egg substitute
¼ cup low-fat milk
1 teaspoon curry powder
3 tablespoons chopped fresh parsley
4 tablespoons (½ stick) butter or margarine
4 large potatoes (about 1¾ pounds), peeled and cut into ½-inch cubes
6 scallions, trimmed, white part and some green, chopped
1 teaspoon salt

1. Lightly beat the eggs with the milk, curry powder, and parsley. Set aside.

2. In a large frying pan, over medium heat, melt the butter or margarine. Add the potatoes and cook over low heat for 10 minutes, or until the potatoes are tender but firm and golden. Stir occasionally.
3. Mix in the scallions and salt and cook for 5 minutes, or until the scallions are crisp-tender.
4. Pour in the egg or egg substitute mixture and cook, stirring, until just set. Do not overcook; the mixture should be creamy.
5. Taste for seasoning, adding more salt if needed.

SERVES 6

Dublin Potato Stew

We often enjoyed this dish in Ireland. The Irish aren't known for their subtle cuisine, but no one can better them in creating stews that feature both lamb for flavor and potatoes for bulk and personality. We prefer to use beef broth in this dish, instead of the water often favored by the Irish.

Serve with a loaf of good Irish soda bread.

6 medium-size potatoes (2 pounds), peeled and cut into ½-inch-thick slices
2 pounds lamb shanks, boned and cut into ½-inch-thick slices
6 medium-size onions, peeled, cut into ½-inch-thick slices
Salt and freshly ground pepper to taste
⅛ teaspoon dried savory
⅛ teaspoon dried oregano
⅛ teaspoon dried thyme
2 cups beef broth

1. In a large casserole, alternate layers of potatoes, meat, and onions. Season each layer lightly with salt, pepper, savory, oregano, and thyme.
2. Pour in the beef broth. Cover and bake in a preheated 325°F oven for 2 hours, or until the meat and potatoes are tender.

SERVES 4

Potatoes Parma Style

The Italians often serve these potatoes with broiled fish.

4 medium-size potatoes (about 1¼ pounds)
6 ounces low-fat cheese, cut into ¼-inch-thick slices
Salt and freshly ground pepper to taste
¼ cup grated Parmesan cheese
2 tablespoons bread crumbs
2 tablespoons butter or margarine

1. Cook the potatoes in their skins in boiling water over medium heat until tender but still somewhat firm. Peel and cut into ¼-inch-thick slices.
2. Butter a large, shallow baking dish. Arrange the potatoes on the bottom in one layer, overlapping, if necessary. Top with the cheese slices, then sprinkle lightly with salt, pepper, Parmesan, and bread crumbs. Dot with butter or margarine and bake in a preheated 400°F oven for 15 minutes.

SERVES 4

Maine Potato Fish Balls

State-of-Mainers love this dish, especially when it's made with their famed mealy potatoes and fresh cod from their cold coastal waters. We often shape these balls into bite-size pieces and serve them as appetizers.

1 pound salt cod
4 large potatoes (about 1¾ pounds)
1 egg white
3 tablespoons butter or margarine, softened
½ teaspoon freshly ground black pepper
Vegetable oil for deep-frying

1. Soak the salt cod in cold water overnight. Drain, then rinse several times in cold water.
2. Cook the potatoes in their skins in boiling water over medium heat until tender. Drain. Dry them over low heat in the same pan. Peel and mash.
3. While the potatoes are cooking, cook the cod in simmering water until tender. Drain well. Mash the cod and set aside.
4. Beat the egg white until foamy.
5. Combine the potatoes, fish, butter or margarine, pepper, and egg white. Beat into a smooth mixture. Refrigerate for 2 hours.
6. Shape mixture into balls. Heat oil to 350°F. Deep-fry balls in hot oil without crowding, until crisp and golden.
7. Drain on paper towels and serve immediately or keep warm in the oven.

Makes thirty 2-inch balls, to serve 4

German Potato-Frankfurt Lunch

6 medium-size potatoes (about 2 pounds)
2 scallions, trimmed and chopped
6 chicken franks
⅓ cup dry white wine (optional)
Water
2 tablespoons oil
2 tablespoons sugar
2 teaspoons flour
1 teaspoon salt
¼ cup cider vinegar
1 tablespoon chopped fresh parsley

1. Cook the potatoes in their skins in boiling water over medium heat. Drain, peel, and dice.
2. In a large serving bowl, combine hot potatoes and scallions. Cover and keep warm.
3. Poach the franks in the wine and ⅓ cup water (or in ⅔ cup water) for 10 minutes. Drain and cut franks into ½-inch-thick slices.
4. In a large frying pan, over medium heat, heat the oil. Add the sliced chicken franks and brown evenly. With a slotted spoon, remove the franks. Reserve the drippings. (If the franks have absorbed all the oil, add another tablespoon to the pan.) Add the sliced franks to the potatoes and keep warm.
5. Add the sugar, flour, and salt to the hot drippings. Stir until smooth and bubbly. Gradually stir in the vinegar and ½ cup water. Cook, stirring constantly, until the sauce thickens.
6. Pour the sauce over the potatoes and franks and blend carefully. Sprinkle with parsley.

SERVES 6

Potatoes with Ground Lamb, Istanbul Style

8 medium-size potatoes (2½ pounds), peeled and cut into slices almost ½ inch thick
3 tablespoons butter or margarine
4 tablespoons olive oil
2 medium-size onions, chopped
1 pound lean ground lamb
½ teaspoon ground cumin
¼ teaspoon ground cinnamon
2 tablespoons chopped fresh mint, or 1 teaspoon dried
2 tablespoons fresh lemon juice
Salt and freshly ground pepper to taste
3 ripe, firm tomatoes, peeled and cut into ½-inch-thick slices
1 cup beef broth
2 tablespoons chopped fresh parsley

1. Dry the potato slices. In a large frying pan, over medium heat, heat half the butter or margarine and oil. Lightly sauté the potato slices, one layer at a time, on both sides. Add more butter or margarine and oil as needed. Arrange the potato slices in one overlapping layer in a casserole.
2. In the same frying pan, cook the onions until soft. Do not brown.
3. Add the ground lamb, cumin, cinnamon, and mint to the onions, and cook, over medium heat, for about 10 minutes, or until the meat loses its pink color and most of the liquid has evaporated.
4. Layer the lamb-and-onion mixture on the potatoes. Sprinkle with lemon juice, salt, and pepper.
5. Arrange the slices of tomatoes on top of the potatoes, sprinkle with salt and pepper, and pour the beef broth

around the edges of the casserole. Cover and bake in a preheated 375°F oven for 30 minutes. Remove the cover and cook 15 minutes longer, or until the potatoes are tender.
6. Sprinkle with the parsley just before serving.

SERVES 6

Old-fashioned Chicken Hash

This makes a satisfying light lunch.

5 cups cubed raw potatoes (2 pounds)
3 cups cubed cooked chicken
2 medium-size onions
1½ teaspoons salt
½ teaspoon freshly ground pepper
⅛ teaspoon thyme
2 tablespoons butter or margarine
1 tablespoon olive oil

1. Put the potatoes, chicken, and onions through a grinder or chop in food processor with steel blade. Blend together in a bowl and season with the salt, pepper, and thyme.
2. In a frying pan heat the butter or margarine and oil. Spoon the potato mixture into the pan, pressing it down with a spatula to form a cakelike patty. Cook until a crust forms on the bottom, stirring occasionally to make sure the hash cooks evenly inside. Turn and cook until crusty brown on the other side.
3. Serve the hash very hot on warm plates.

SERVES 6

Hoppelpoppel

We first sampled this traditional German dish at the home of friends in Munich. Low-cholesterol substitute can be used in place of the fresh eggs.

8 eggs
2 tablespoons milk
1 teaspoon salt
½ teaspoon freshly ground pepper
1 tablespoon minced fresh chives
4 medium-size potatoes (1¼ pounds)
3 tablespoons butter or margarine
2 cups diced lean ham (½ pound)
3 medium-size onions, chopped

1. In a large bowl, beat together the eggs, milk, salt, pepper, and chives. Set aside.
2. Cook the potatoes in their skins in boiling water over medium heat until barely tender. Drain and dry over low heat in the same pan. Peel and cut into ¼-inch-thick slices. (The slices should be firm.)
3. In a large frying pan, over medium heat, melt the butter or margarine. Add the ham and cook until almost crisp. Remove the ham and drain on paper towels.
4. Add the onions and more butter or margarine, if needed, to the frying pan and cook for 5 minutes, or until soft. Do not brown. Add the potato slices, cooking over medium heat for 10 minutes. Turn to brown evenly.
5. Sprinkle the ham over the potatoes, then pour in the egg mixture to cover all evenly. Cook over low heat for 8 minutes, shaking the pan once the eggs begin to set to prevent sticking, or lift in several places with a spatula. The eggs should be well set, but still somewhat moist.

6. Place a warm plate, larger than the pan, over the frying pan. Holding both together, quickly turn pan to dislodge the egg mixture onto the plate, brown-side up. Serve hot, in wedges.

SERVES 4

Irish Breast of Veal with Lemon Potatoes

Stuffing

2 tablespoons butter or margarine
1 medium-size onion, chopped
½ pound lean ground beef
½ pound mushrooms, chopped
One 10-ounce package frozen chopped spinach, thawed and squeezed dry
½ cup grated low-fat cheese
½ teaspoon dried basil
Salt and freshly ground pepper

1 breast of veal, boned (4 pounds with bone, 2 pounds if boned)
1 cup beef broth
2 onions, cut into chunks
6 medium-size potatoes (about 2 pounds), scrubbed and cut into chunks
1 teaspoon dried thyme
1 teaspoon grated lemon rind
Paprika
Lemon slices

1. Melt the butter or margarine in a frying pan, over medium heat. Add the onion and beef and sauté for 10 minutes. Transfer to a bowl.
2. In the same pan, cook the mushrooms until the moisture evaporates. Add the mushrooms to the meat mixture along with the spinach.
3. Blend the cheese, basil, ¾ teaspoon salt, and ¼ teaspoon pepper into the mixture. Taste for seasoning. Set stuffing aside.
4. Lay the veal flat, sprinkle lightly with salt and pepper, and spread the stuffing on the center third of the meat. Fold over both ends and tie with string. Place veal in a roasting pan and add the broth. Cover the pan with a lid or foil and bake in a preheated 325°F oven for 1½ hours. Remove cover occasionally and baste with pan juices.
5. Sprinkle the onion and potato chunks with thyme, lemon rind, and paprika, then add to the roasting pan, stirring to coat with pan drippings. Bake for another 45 minutes, or until the veal and potatoes are tender, stirring the potatoes occasionally.
6. Serve veal and potatoes garnished with lemon slices.

SERVES 6

Jambota

This piquant dish is an interesting way to use leftover poultry or seafood.

Butter or margarine
Olive oil
3 garlic cloves, crushed
2 medium-size onions, thinly sliced

4 medium-size potatoes (1¼ pounds), peeled and sliced medium thick
1 small red pepper, cored and sliced medium thick
1 small green pepper, cored and sliced medium thick
2 cups cooked chicken, turkey, or seafood
Salt and freshly ground pepper to taste

1. Heat 2 tablespoons butter or margarine and 1 tablespoon oil in a frying pan, over medium heat. Cook the garlic until golden. Discard garlic.
2. Add the onions to the frying pan and cook until golden. Transfer the onions to a large bowl.
3. Add more butter or margarine and oil, if necessary, then cook the potatoes just until golden on both sides, but still firm. Add to the bowl.
4. Stir-fry the peppers lightly in the frying pan and add to the bowl.
5. Blend the cooked chicken, turkey, or seafood into the potatoes and season with salt and pepper.
6. Butter a 1½-quart casserole, and spoon in the *jambota* mixture. Bake, uncovered, in a preheated 350°F oven for 15 minutes, or until the potatoes are tender but the peppers are still firm. If necessary, remove the peppers before the potatoes are cooked, then return them to the casserole.

SERVES 4

Lancashire Hotpot

We first sampled this unique dish on a trip to England. Accustomed as we are to eating our oysters raw, we suspected that the oysters would be overdone and tough. But the addition of the shellfish lends this dish a surprisingly delicate flavor, transforming it into a culinary experience. Naturally, the firm base and the crown of glory are made of potatoes.

1½ pounds leg of lamb
7 medium-size Idaho potatoes (about 2¼ pounds), peeled and cut into ¼-inch-thick slices
Salt and freshly ground pepper to taste
4 small onions, thinly sliced
4 lamb kidneys, cored, soaked in salt water, rinsed well in cold water, and thinly sliced
12 (or more) shucked oysters
1½ cups beef broth
2 tablespoons butter or margarine, melted

1. Cut lamb into ½-inch-thick slices, about the size of the potato pieces.
2. Butter a deep 2-quart casserole. Layer with half the potatoes and all the lamb. Sprinkle lightly with salt and pepper.
3. Arrange another layer of half the onions, then top with the kidneys. Sprinkle with salt and pepper.
4. Layer the oysters on top of the kidneys. Add the remaining onions and end with a layer of potatoes, lightly seasoning with salt and pepper.
5. Pour in the beef broth. Drizzle the melted butter or margarine over the potatoes. Bake, covered, in a preheated 350°F oven for 1½ hours.
6. Remove the cover and bake for 30 minutes longer, or until the potatoes are crisply brown.

SERVES 6

Maria Luisa's Timballo

3 eggs, or cholesterol-free egg substitute
1 cup flour
1 teaspoon salt
6 medium-size potatoes (about 2 pounds)
6 tablespoons olive oil
½ pound low-fat mozzarella, thinly sliced
3 tablespoons butter or margarine
Salt and freshly ground pepper to taste
¼ pound prosciutto, julienned
3 tablespoons grated Parmesan cheese
2 tablespoons butter or margarine, melted

1. In a shallow bowl, lightly beat the eggs. Set aside. In another bowl, blend the flour and salt together and reserve.
2. Cook the potatoes in their skins in boiling water over medium heat until barely tender. Drain and dry over low heat in the same pan. Peel and cut into ¼-inch-thick slices. (The slices should be reasonably firm.)
3. Sprinkle seasoned flour onto a sheet of wax paper. Dip the potato slices into the beaten eggs, then dredge with the flour.
4. Heat the olive oil in a frying pan. Over medium heat, evenly brown the potato slices in the oil, adding more oil, if needed. Drain on paper towels.
5. Lightly butter a casserole. Layer the potato slices, covering each layer with the mozzarella, dotting with butter or margarine, and seasoning with salt and pepper. The top layer should be cheese.
6. Bake, uncovered, in a preheated 375°F oven for 15 minutes, or until the potatoes are tender and the cheese has melted. Remove from oven.

7. Lattice the top with the prosciutto strips, then sprinkle with Parmesan and melted butter or margarine. Slip under the broiler for 1 minute and serve immediately.

Serves 6

Mariners' Scalloped Potatoes

This dish is a favorite of some people we know who live by or work on the sea. We first sampled it at the home of a seaman, a captain of his own craft, who did most of his fishing in the area near the Isles of Shoals, 10 miles from the coast of Maine. The combination of mealy Maine potatoes and the sweet bay scallops has become one of our all-time favorite meals.

Don't let all the "steps" bother you; this is easy to prepare. It may be served in one large baking dish, but the individual ramekins make for a more interesting presentation.

Step 1. Potatoes

8 medium-size (2½ pounds) potatoes
6 tablespoons (¾ stick) butter or margarine, softened
2 eggs, lightly beaten
Salt and freshly ground pepper to taste
½ cup low-fat milk

1. Cook the potatoes in their skins in boiling water over medium heat until tender. Drain and dry over low heat in the same pan. Peel and put through a potato ricer or food mill.
2. In a large bowl, combine the riced potatoes, butter or

margarine, eggs, salt, pepper, and milk. Beat with an electric mixer until smooth and fluffy. Set the mixture aside.

Step 2. Vegetables

2 tablespoons butter or margarine
¼ cup minced shallots
¼ cup chopped celery
½ pound small fresh mushrooms, thinly sliced
2 tablespoons chopped fresh parsley
Salt and freshly ground pepper to taste

Melt the butter or margarine in a saucepan, over medium heat. Add the shallots and celery and cook until soft. Do not brown. Add the mushrooms and cook for 3 minutes. Stir in the parsley, salt, and pepper. Set aside.

Step 3. Scallops

1½ pounds bay scallops, or sea scallops cut in quarters
¾ cup dry white wine or clam juice, enough to just cover
Pinch of dried thyme

Place the scallops, wine or clam juice, and thyme in a saucepan and poach for 4 minutes. Remove the scallops with a slotted spoon and set aside, reserving ½ cup poaching liquid for Step 4.

Step 4. Sauce

4 tablespoons (½ stick) butter or margarine
¼ cup flour
2½ cups milk
1 teaspoon Worcestershire sauce
10 tablespoons grated cheese, preferably Gruyère
Salt and freshly ground pepper to taste

1. Melt the butter or margarine in a deep saucepan over medium heat. Gradually add in the flour, stirring con-

stantly until you have a thick, golden paste. Gradually stir in the reserved ½ cup poaching liquid and the milk, continuing to stir until the sauce is medium-thick and smooth. Add the Worcestershire sauce, 4 tablespoons cheese, salt, and pepper, stirring until the cheese has melted.

2. Add the poached scallops from Step 3 and the vegetables from Step 2 to the sauce, blending well. Divide among 6 individual ramekins. Evenly spread equal amounts of the beaten potatoes from Step 1 over each, sprinkling the top of each with 1 tablespoon of cheese.

3. Place the ramekins on a baking sheet in a preheated 400°F oven for 30 minutes, or until the sauce bubbles. Remove from the oven and place under a broiler until the tops are crispy golden.

Serves 6

Potato Meat Loaf

The addition of grated potato not only gives this meat loaf a superb flavor but keeps it moist and helps to prevent it from falling apart when cut. The potatoes also give body and make each portion go a lot further. Do not overcook the meat loaf—a moist texture is part of its appeal.

2 tablespoons butter or margarine
1 medium-size onion, chopped
2 medium-size potatoes (¾ pound), grated into cold water
1½ pounds lean ground round
1 egg, lightly beaten
1½ teaspoons salt
½ teaspoon freshly ground pepper

2 tablespoons tomato sauce
1 tablespoon chopped raisins
3 tablespoons freshly grated Romano cheese

1. Sauté the onion in butter or margarine until soft. Do not brown.
2. Drain the potatoes and, in a large bowl, combine with the onion and the remaining ingredients. Blend well.
3. Butter a 9-by-5-by-3-inch loaf pan. With your hands, mold the meat mixture into a loaf and place it in the pan. Smooth and mold it to conform to the pan.
4. Bake, uncovered, in a preheated 375°F oven for 50 minutes. Test with a toothpick. If it withdraws clean the meat loaf is done.

SERVES 5 TO 6

New Zealand Potato-Lamb Pot

This dish is simple, quick, inexpensive, and tasty—virtues of a perfect meal anywhere.

2 tablespoons butter or margarine
1 tablespoon olive oil
1 pound diced lean lamb shoulder
4 large potatoes (about 1¾ pounds), peeled and cut into ½-inch cubes
6 medium-size onions, quartered
6 hard-boiled eggs, peeled and quartered (optional)
Salt and freshly ground pepper to taste
One 10½-ounce can mushroom soup blended with 1 cup water
⅓ cup bread crumbs

1. Heat the butter or margarine and oil in a skillet, over medium heat. Brown the diced lamb in the oil. Set aside.
2. Lightly butter a 2-quart casserole. Layer the lamb, potatoes, onions, and eggs, if desired, in the dish, ending with potatoes. Season with salt and pepper.
3. Pour the soup-water blend over the potato-lamb mixture. Sprinkle with the bread crumbs.
4. Bake, uncovered, in a preheated 350°F oven for 40 to 50 minutes, or until the top is crusty brown and the potatoes and lamb are tender. (If the top gets too brown before the potatoes and lamb are tender, cover the casserole loosely with foil.)

Serves 4 to 6

Potato-Shrimp Pizza

Sometimes it's nice to try a variation on the classic pizza. Here's one with a different slant—but still in the same family.

6 medium-size potatoes (2 pounds)
Salt and freshly ground pepper to taste
4 tablespoons (½ stick) butter or margarine
1 tablespoon olive oil
2 medium-size onions, thinly sliced
2 garlic cloves, thinly sliced
1 green pepper, seeded, cored, and cut into ¼-inch strips
⅛ teaspoon red pepper flakes
12 pitted small green olives, halved
1 tablespoon capers, rinsed and drained

1 pound medium-size shrimp (about 32 to the pound), shelled and deveined

1. Cook the potatoes in their skins in boiling water over medium heat until tender. Drain and dry in the same pan over low heat. Peel, then mash into a smooth purée and season with salt and pepper.
2. Melt 2 tablespoons of butter or margarine. Set aside.
3. Generously butter a large, very shallow baking dish (a jelly-roll pan is perfect). Spread the potatoes over the bottom in a ⅜-inch-thick layer (it's not necessary for the potatoes to cover the entire bottom). Drizzle the melted butter or margarine on top and bake in a preheated 425°F oven for 40 minutes, or until the bottom is crispy and brown and the top golden.
4. Meanwhile heat the remaining 2 tablespoons butter or margarine and the oil in a frying pan. Over medium heat, cook the onions, garlic, and green pepper until crisp-tender. Stir in the red pepper flakes, salt, pepper, olives, capers, and shrimp. Cook just until the shrimp turn pink. Do not overcook.
5. Spoon the shrimp-vegetable mixture over the baked potato purée and serve.

SERVES 4

Frittata

This classic dish calls for 8 fresh eggs (egg substitutes just won't work here). If you can, make this dish for a special occasion. It's a great brunch or late supper treat.

4 small new potatoes (½ pound)
2 tablespoons butter or margarine
2 tablespoons olive oil
1 small red onion, thinly sliced
1 small green pepper, cored and thinly sliced
1 small red pepper, cored and thinly sliced
1 small zucchini, unpeeled and thinly sliced
Salt and freshly ground pepper to taste
8 eggs
6 tablespoons grated Parmesan cheese
2 tablespoons minced fresh parsley
½ cup minced prosciutto
½ teaspoon dried oregano
Dash hot pepper sauce

1. Cook the potatoes in their skins in boiling water over medium heat until tender but firm. Drain and dry in the same pan over low heat. Peel, cool, and slice. Set aside.
2. Heat the butter or margarine and oil in an ovenproof 12-inch frying pan. Cook the onion, peppers, and zucchini until tender but not limp. Season with salt and pepper.
3. With a wire whisk, beat the eggs in a large bowl until fluffy. Add half the Parmesan, the parsley, prosciutto, oregano, and hot sauce. Stir.
4. Add the potatoes to the other vegetables in the frying pan and heat. Pour the egg mixture over the vegetables. Cook about 1 minute, or until the *frittata* begins to set. Sprinkle 3 tablespoons Parmesan on top. Bake in a preheated 350°F oven for 15 minutes or until the eggs have set and the top is puffed.

SERVES 8

Pasquale's Potato-Turkey Pie

7 medium-size potatoes (2¼ pounds)
1 teaspoon salt
½ teaspoon freshly ground pepper
3 tablespoons butter or margarine
¼ cup freshly grated Parmesan cheese
⅛ teaspoon ground mace
½ to 1 cup milk
2 tablespoons olive oil
6 low-fat sweet Italian turkey sausages

1. Cook the potatoes in their skins in boiling water over medium heat until tender. Drain and dry over low heat in the same pan. Peel and rice the potatoes or put through a food mill.
2. Place the riced potatoes in a large bowl. With a wire whisk, beat in the salt, pepper, butter or margarine, Parmesan, mace, and enough milk to make a smooth and fluffy mixture. Taste for seasoning.
3. In a frying pan, heat the olive oil. Remove the casings from the sausages and crumble the meat. Add to the oil and cook for 15 minutes, breaking up the mixture as it cooks. Drain, then mix into the potatoes, blending well.
4. Lightly butter a deep casserole and fill with the potato-sausage mixture, smoothing the top in a cakelike fashion.
5. Bake, uncovered, in a preheated 375°F oven for 15 minutes, or until the top is crusty brown.

SERVES 6

Potato Pastitsio

This classic Greek dish is usually made with pasta, but sometimes potatoes are used instead. We've tried both—it's a standoff.

7 medium-size potatoes (2¼ pounds)
2 tablespoons olive oil
1 pound lean ground beef
4 medium-size onions, chopped
3 tablespoons tomato sauce
3 tablespoons dry white wine (optional)
Salt and freshly ground pepper to taste
2 eggs, lightly beaten
4 tablespoons finely crumbled feta cheese
⅛ teaspoon ground mace
¼ cup milk beaten with 1 egg
¼ cup bread crumbs
2 tablespoons butter or margarine

1. Cook the potatoes in their skins in boiling water over medium heat until tender. Drain and dry over low heat in the same pan. Peel and rice or put through a food mill.
2. In a saucepan, heat the oil and lightly brown the meat with the onions. Drain off any fat that accumulates. Stir in the tomato sauce, wine, if desired, salt, and pepper. Cover and simmer for 15 minutes. Remove the cover and simmer until all the liquid has evaporated.
3. In a large bowl, combine the potatoes, eggs, 2 tablespoons feta, and mace. Season with salt and pepper. Blend well.
4. Lightly butter a large baking dish. Layer it with half of the potatoes and cover with all of the meat and onion mixture. Top with the remaining potatoes. Pour the milk and

egg mixture over the potatoes. Sprinkle with bread crumbs and the remaining feta. Dot with the butter or margarine.
5. Bake, uncovered, in a preheated 350°F oven for 25 minutes, or until the cheese melts and the top browns.

SERVES 6

Lentil-Potato Poach

1 pound dried lentils
1 large carrot, scraped and chopped
1 large celery stalk, scraped and chopped
2 garlic cloves, minced
Pinch of thyme
2 medium-size onions, chopped
5 tablespoons olive oil
Salt and freshly ground pepper to taste
3 cups Chicken Broth (page 22), or canned
4 large potatoes (about 1¾ pounds), peeled and cut into walnut-size pieces
2 tablespoons chopped fresh broadleaf parsley
1 teaspoon paprika

1. Rinse the lentils well and drain. Place in a deep pot along with the carrot, celery, garlic, thyme, half the onions, 3 tablespoons olive oil, a good sprinkle of salt and pepper, and the chicken broth. Bring to a boil, reduce to a simmer, cover, and cook for 20 minutes.
2. Add the potatoes. Add additional broth, if needed to cover the potatoes. Cover, and cook for 15 minutes, or until the potatoes are tender.
3. In a saucepan, heat the remaining 2 tablespoons olive

oil, then add the remaining onions and the parsley. Cook until the onions are soft. Do not brown. Stir in the paprika and blend into the potato-lentil pot. Simmer, uncovered, for 10 minutes. Taste for seasoning and serve.

Serves 4

Pork Pie with Potato-Cheese Crust

6 medium-size potatoes (2 pounds)
1½ cups grated sharp Cheddar cheese (6 ounces)
3 tablespoons butter or margarine
2 medium-size onions, thinly sliced
5 medium-size firm mushrooms, thinly sliced
2 tablespoons flour
1 teaspoon salt
½ teaspoon freshly ground pepper
⅛ teaspoon cayenne
1½ cups beef broth
2 cups diced, cooked lean pork

1. Cook the potatoes in their skins in boiling water over medium heat until tender. Drain. Dry them over low heat in the same pan. Peel and mash.
2. Blend the Cheddar into the hot mashed potatoes. Stir until the cheese melts.
3. In a saucepan, melt the butter or margarine and cook the onions for 5 minutes. Add the mushrooms and cook for another 2 minutes. Stir in the flour, salt, pepper, and cayenne, mixing well. Pour in the broth, a little at a time, stirring and simmering until the sauce thickens. Add the pork, blending well. Taste for seasoning.
4. Place the mixture in a buttered 2-quart casserole.

Spread and smooth the potato-cheese mixture on top and bake, uncovered, in a preheated 350°F oven for 25 minutes, or until the top is golden.

SERVES 4

Quiche Barbara M. Valbona

This makes an excellent luncheon or quick supper dish.

9-inch pie shell
3 eggs, slightly beaten, or cholesterol-free egg substitute
1⅓ cups milk
½ cup chopped onion (1 small)
1 medium potato, thinly sliced (about 1 cup)
2 tablespoons butter or margarine
½ cup chopped prosciutto
Salt and freshly ground pepper to taste
1 cup shredded, low-fat sharp Cheddar cheese (about 4 ounces)

1. Bake the pie shell in a preheated 350°F oven for 10 minutes.
2. Blend together beaten eggs and milk. Set aside.
3. In a frying pan, cook the onion and potato in the butter or margarine until golden. Add the prosciutto, salt, and pepper. Spread the mixture on the bottom of the pie shell. Sprinkle the Cheddar over the top, then pour in the milk mixture.
4. Bake in a preheated 375°F oven for 30 to 35 minutes or until set and golden.

SERVES 6

Potato Ring

This is a dramatic and different way to serve potatoes and meat as a meal-in-one. Creamed meat dishes—chicken, veal, dried beef with peas—are perfect to serve within the potato ring, although we favor chicken.

5 large potatoes (about 2¼ pounds)
5 tablespoons butter or margarine, softened
4 eggs, lightly beaten, or cholesterol-free egg substitute
½ pound cooked chicken, finely chopped
1 tablespoon minced fresh broadleaf parsley
Salt and freshly ground pepper to taste
½ teaspoon Dijon mustard
Bread crumbs

1. Cook the potatoes in their skins in boiling water over medium heat until tender. Drain and dry over low heat in the same pan. Peel the potatoes and put through a ricer or food mill into a large bowl. Beat in 3 tablespoons butter or margarine, the eggs, chicken, parsley, salt, pepper, and mustard.
2. Butter a 1½-quart ring mold. Sprinkle the inside with bread crumbs and invert to remove excess. Spoon in the potato mixture. Dot the top with the remaining 2 tablespoons butter or margarine.
3. Bake, uncovered, in a preheated 350°F oven for 25 minutes, or until set and golden on top. Invert potato ring onto a serving dish, and fill the ring with a creamed dish of your choice.

SERVES 6

Potato and Rolled Chicken Breast Casserole

3 medium-size potatoes (about 1 pound)
4 tablespoons (½ stick) butter or margarine, softened
½ cup milk
Salt and freshly ground pepper to taste
4 halves chicken breast, skinned, boned, and flattened with a mallet or rolling pin
2 slices prosciutto, cut in half
1 teaspoon chopped fresh parsley
½ teaspoon dried sage
2 medium-size carrots, scraped and coarsely grated
1 scallion, trimmed and finely chopped
1 pound Swiss chard, stems removed and coarsely chopped
2 tablespoons freshly grated Parmesan cheese

1. Cook the potatoes in their skins in boiling water over medium heat until tender. Drain and dry over low heat in the same pan. Peel, then mash by hand or with an electric mixer. Add 2 tablespoons butter or margarine, the milk, salt, and pepper to the potatoes. Mix well. Set aside.
2. Top each chicken breast half with a piece of prosciutto and sprinkle with some parsley, sage, salt, and pepper. Roll up each breast jelly-roll fashion and secure with string or toothpicks.
3. In a heavy frying pan, melt 2 tablespoons butter or margarine. Add the chicken rolls and cook until evenly brown, about 15 minutes.
4. In a heavy saucepan with a tight-fitting lid, cook the carrots and scallion in 1 inch of salted water, covered, for 2 minutes. Add the chard and cook for 4 minutes, or until

the vegetables are tender. Drain well and season with salt and pepper.

5. Arrange the chard mixture in the bottom of a shallow, buttered 2-quart casserole, and spread the potato mixture evenly on top. Place the chicken rolls on the potatoes and sprinkle with the Parmesan.

6. Bake, uncovered, in a preheated 375°F oven 30 minutes, or until the chicken is tender. Remove the string or toothpicks before serving.

Serves 4

Potato Roll Dinner

Here's a deliciously different one-dish meal, a guest-grabber that will have you at the typewriter sending out recipes to one and all.

4 medium-size potatoes (1¼ pounds)
6 tablespoons (¾ stick) butter or margarine
1 tablespoon chopped fresh chives
Salt and freshly ground pepper to taste
2 medium-size onions, chopped
1 pound lean ground round
½ pound lean ground pork
2 tablespoons freshly grated Parmesan cheese
2 tablespoons minced golden raisins
½ teaspoon dried oregano
½ cup bread crumbs
2 eggs, lightly beaten, or cholesterol-free substitute
1 tablespoon olive oil
Flour (optional)
Beef broth (optional)

1. Cook the potatoes in their skins in boiling water over medium heat until tender. Drain. Dry them over low heat in the same pan. Peel and mash.
2. Add 2 tablespoons butter or margarine, chives, and salt and pepper to taste to the mashed potatoes. Blend well and set aside.
3. In a saucepan, melt 2 tablespoons butter or margarine and cook the onions for 5 minutes, or until soft. Do not brown. In a large bowl, combine the onions and all the remaining ingredients, except the potatoes, the remaining butter or margarine, and olive oil, mixing well.
4. Spread out and oil a large piece of wax paper. Reserve ½ cup of the meat mixture. Spread the remaining meat mixture on the wax paper, making a 10-by-7-by-½-inch rectangle. Mold the meat into a solid cake. Spread the mashed potatoes on top, smoothing them evenly with the flat of a knife.
5. Lifting up the wax paper, roll the mixture jelly-roll fashion as tightly as possible, to completely encase the potatoes. If there are any holes, patch with the reserved meat. If not, pat the reserved meat onto the ends of the roll.
6. Carefully slide the roll off the paper onto a shallow, lightly buttered baking pan. Bake, uncovered, in a preheated 350°F oven for 1 hour.
7. Heat the remaining 2 tablespoons butter or margarine with the olive oil and baste the meat-potato roll with it.
8. Remove roll from oven and let sit for 5 minutes. Use a sharp serrated knife to slice the roll for serving. You can make a brown sauce or gravy by adding a little flour and some beef broth to the pan, if desired.

SERVES 6

Potato–Salmon Custard

2 large potatoes (about 1 pound)
Salt and freshly ground pepper to taste
One 15½-ounce can red salmon, drained, 2 tablespoons liquid reserved
1 tablespoon butter or margarine
1 celery stalk, scraped and finely chopped
6 scallions, trimmed and finely chopped
3 eggs, lightly beaten, or cholesterol-free egg substitute
2½ cups milk
½ teaspoon dry mustard
1 tablespoon chopped fresh dill, or 1 teaspoon dried

1. Cook the potatoes in their skins in boiling water over medium heat until tender. Drain and dry in the same pan over low heat. Peel the potatoes and cut into ¼-inch-thick slices.
2. Butter a 1½-quart shallow baking dish and arrange the potato slices in a single overlapping layer. Sprinkle lightly with salt and pepper.
3. Remove the skin and bones from the salmon and flake with a fork. Layer over the potatoes.
4. In a frying pan, heat the butter or margarine. Cook the celery and half the scallions for 3 minutes, or until just soft.
5. In a bowl, combine the eggs, milk, mustard, dill, the reserved salmon liquid, and the cooked scallions and celery. Season with salt and pepper, mix well, then carefully spoon over the salmon-potato mixture.
6. Bake, uncovered, in a preheated 350°F oven for 30 to 40 minutes, until set (a knife inserted 1 inch from center should come out clean). If the top browns before it sets, cover loosely with foil.

7. Sprinkle the remaining scallions around the edge of the dish and serve.

SERVES 4

Scalloped Potatoes with Ham

This favorite American supper dish can be made using chopped or sliced cooked meat or vegetables such as sliced celery or chopped red or green sweet peppers. But this version is classic.

2 tablespoons butter or margarine
3 medium-size onions, chopped
¼ cup flour
½ teaspoon salt
1 teaspoon celery salt
½ teaspoon freshly ground pepper
2 cups low-fat milk
1 cup grated very sharp cheese, preferably Cheddar
6 medium-size potatoes (about 2 pounds), peeled and cut into ¼-inch-thick slices
2 cups diced or wafer-thin sliced lean, cooked ham

1. Melt the butter or margarine in a saucepan over medium heat. Add the onions and sauté until soft. Do not brown. Stir in the flour, salt, celery salt, and pepper, blending thoroughly. Reduce heat to low.
2. Gradually stir in the milk, stirring constantly until the sauce is smooth and thick. Stir in the cheese and cook, stirring, until melted. Taste for seasoning.
3. Butter a 2-quart casserole and alternate layers of pota-

toes, ham, and sauce, ending with a layer of potatoes covered with the sauce.
4. Bake, covered, in a preheated 375°F oven for 45 minutes. Remove the cover and bake for 20 minutes longer, or until the potatoes are tender and the top is golden brown.

Serves 6

Shepherd's Pie #1

The so-called "classic" shepherd's pie comes from Scotland. It was frugally built around leftover lamb and potatoes.

3 tablespoons butter or margarine
1 large white onion, minced
2 tablespoons flour
1½ cups beef broth
4 cups cubed, lean cooked lamb, beef, or veal
Dash Worcestershire sauce
2 tablespoons minced fresh parsley
Salt and freshly ground pepper to taste
Pinch of ground mace
3 cups mashed potatoes
3 tablespoons grated low-fat sharp cheese

1. Heat 2 tablespoons butter or margarine in a large saucepan. Add the onion and cook until soft. Do not brown. Stir in the flour, then gradually add the beef broth. Stir until smooth. Blend in the meat cubes, Worcestershire sauce, parsley, salt, pepper, and mace.
2. Butter a 2-quart casserole. Spoon in the meat mixture,

then cover with an even layer of the mashed potatoes. Dot with the remaining tablespoon of butter or margarine and sprinkle with the cheese.
3. Bake, uncovered, in a preheated 400°F oven for 30 minutes, or until heated through and the top is golden.

SERVES 6

Shepherd's Pie #2

The French have their own version of shepherd's pie.

1 pound cold boiled beef
4 slices lean Canadian bacon
5 medium-size potatoes (1¾ pounds)
4 tablespoons (½ stick) butter or margarine
⅓ cup warm milk
Salt and freshly ground pepper to taste
4 medium-size onions, peeled and chopped
2 tablespoons chopped broadleaf parsley
⅓ cup bread crumbs
2 tablespoons milk
1 egg, lightly beaten
3 tablespoons grated Swiss cheese

1. Grind together the beef and bacon. Set aside.
2. Cook the potatoes in their skins in boiling water over medium heat. Drain and dry over low heat in the same pan. Peel and mash with 2 tablespoons butter or margarine and the warm milk. Season with salt and pepper. Set aside.
3. In a large saucepan, over medium heat, melt the

remaining 2 tablespoons butter or margarine and cook the onions for 5 minutes. Do not brown.
4. In a bowl, mix the ground meats and parsley and season with salt and pepper. Make a paste with the bread crumbs and milk and add to the ground meat mixture.
5. Stir the meat mixture into the saucepan with the onions. Mix well and cook, simmering, for 3 minutes. Remove from heat and cool. Blend in the egg.
6. Lightly butter a 1½-quart casserole. Put the meat mixture into it and cover with the mashed potatoes, smoothing the top. Sprinkle with the cheese and bake, uncovered, in a preheated 400°F oven for 20 minutes, or until thoroughly heated and golden brown.

Serves 4

Potato Stew with Chicken and Shallots

5 tablespoons butter or margarine
1 tablespoon olive oil
5 medium-size potatoes (1¾ pounds), peeled and cut into 1-inch cubes
12 shallots, or very small white onions, peeled
Salt and freshly ground pepper to taste
½ pound small mushrooms, halved
1 bay leaf
4 chicken breast halves, boned and skinned
¼ cup brandy (optional)
2 cups Chicken Broth (page 22), or canned
2 tablespoons chopped fresh parsley

1. In a frying pan, heat 2 tablespoons butter or margarine and the oil. Add the potatoes and shallots or onions and season with salt and pepper. Cook, stirring, for 10 minutes, or until the potatoes are golden.
2. Remove the potatoes and shallots or onions with a slotted spoon and mix with the mushrooms. Layer the mixture on the bottom of a buttered casserole. Lay the bay leaf on top.
3. In the same frying pan, add the remaining 3 tablespoons of butter or margarine. Brown the chicken breasts on both sides, seasoning with salt and pepper. Remove from the pan and cut into bite-size pieces. Arrange the chicken on top of the potato mixture.
4. Pour the brandy (or use some broth) into the frying pan and, stirring and scraping the bottom of the pan, simmer to allow most of the liquid to evaporate. Pour in the broth and simmer 1 minute. Spoon the broth over the contents of the casserole and bake, covered, in a preheated 350°F oven for 20 minutes.
5. Remove the cover from the casserole and cook for another 15 minutes, or until the chicken and potatoes are tender. Sprinkle with the parsley just before serving.

SERVES 4

Potatoes with Poached Duck

The French often combine duck with turnips, which may seem an odd couple. But they also pair the bird with potatoes, which seems perfect—and it is.

One 5-pound duck, cut into serving pieces
1 large peeled, quartered onion, 1 quarter stuck with a whole clove
3 cups Chicken Broth (page 22), or canned
1 teaspoon salt
½ teaspoon freshly ground pepper
2 teaspoons chopped fresh thyme, or ½ teaspoon dried
4 large celery stalks, scraped and cut into 1-inch pieces
4 medium-size carrots, scraped and cut into bite-size pieces
5 medium-size potatoes (1¾ pounds), peeled and quartered

1. Poach the duck in water to cover, along with the onion, for 25 minutes. Drain thoroughly and discard the onion.
2. In a large pot, place the poached duck and the remaining ingredients, except the potatoes. Cover, bring to a boil, and simmer over medium heat for 20 minutes. Skim off any surface fat.
3. Add the potatoes, cover, and simmer for 30 minutes, or until the duck and the vegetables are tender. Transfer duck and vegetables to a hot dish and keep warm.
4. Over high heat, reduce the liquid remaining in the pot by two-thirds.
5. Remove the skin from the duck. On a hot, deep serving dish, arrange the duck pieces, surrounded by the vegetables. Spoon the hot liquid over all.

Serves 4

6

Side Dishes and Accompaniments

YOU WANT TO FORGET ABOUT INFLATION, THE SHRINKING dollar, and the complicated world in general. So, you invite a couple of special friends to dinner and splurge on a nice fillet of beef. What wine should you serve, what vegetable, and, oh yes, what potato dish? Potato and fillet of beef go together like moon and June.

What about Parmesan Potatoes (page 141), spicy and hot? What about the combination of New Potatoes, Swiss Chard, and Chick-peas (page 139)? Or flavorful Swedish Anchovy Potatoes (page 144)?

You may worry that these dishes sound too complicated or require too much expertise. Read on—this chapter is designed for people in a potato rut. It's structured to help them come up with new, easy-to-prepare, innovative, imaginative potato dishes for both elegant dining and family meals.

Potatoes Baked in Ale

3 medium-size onions, thinly sliced
Salt and freshly ground pepper to taste
5 medium-size potatoes (1¾ pounds), peeled and thinly sliced
1 cup ale
2 tablespoons butter or margarine
½ cup milk

1. Arrange a layer of onions in a buttered 1½-quart oblong baking dish. Lightly season with salt and pepper. Cover with a layer of potatoes, again seasoning lightly. Repeat, ending with a layer of potatoes. Pour the ale along the sides of the casserole and dot the top with butter or margarine.
2. Bake, uncovered, in a preheated 400°F oven for 10 minutes. Reduce the heat to 350°F and cook 40 minutes longer. Pour the milk over the top and cook for another 10 minutes, or until the potatoes are tender and cooked through.

Serves 4

Potato Balls with Curry Sauce

5 medium-size potatoes (1¾ pounds)
4 scallions, white part and some green, trimmed and minced
Salt to taste
¼ teaspoon chili powder

1 egg, lightly beaten
Vegetable oil

Curry Sauce

1 tablespoon butter or margarine
1 tablespoon vegetable oil
1 medium-size onion, chopped
2 teaspoons curry powder
3 large, ripe tomatoes, peeled, seeded, and chopped
1 cup Chicken Broth (page 22), or canned
Salt to taste
¾ cup low-fat yogurt
2 tablespoons chopped fresh coriander or parsley

1. Cook the potatoes in their skins in boiling water over medium heat until tender. Drain. Dry them over low heat in the same pan. Peel and mash.
2. In a large bowl, combine the potatoes, scallions, salt, chili powder, and egg. Form the mixture into 1-inch balls.
3. Heat the oil to 350°F in a deep-fryer or an electric fryer. With a slotted spoon, place a few of the balls at a time in the hot oil. Cook for 5 to 10 minutes, or until golden. Remove with a slotted spoon, drain on paper towels, and keep warm in a 250°F oven until all are cooked.
4. To make the curry sauce, heat the butter or margarine and oil in a frying pan. Add the onion and cook for 3 minutes, or until soft. Do not brown. Stir in the curry powder and cook another 2 minutes.
5. Add the tomatoes, broth, and salt. Simmer for 15 minutes, uncovered, or until the sauce thickens. (This part of the sauce can be prepared in advance.)
6. Cool slightly and stir in the yogurt. Remove the potato balls from the oven and add to the sauce. Heat through, but do not boil.
7. Serve with coriander or parsley sprinkled on top.

MAKES 24 BALLS, TO SERVE 6

Basil-Baked New Potatoes en Papillote

We like to serve these potatoes, 6 to a serving, with broiled fresh fish. Try to get *tiny* potatoes—if you can't, get the smallest possible, then extend cooking time accordingly.

36 tiny new unpeeled potatoes (about 2 pounds), washed and dried
1½ teaspoons salt
3 tablespoons butter or margarine
5 fresh basil leaves, washed and dried

1. Place the potatoes on a large sheet of parchment paper or foil, sprinkle with salt, and dot with butter or margarine. Bury the basil leaves among the potatoes. Wrap the paper or foil tightly around the potatoes, keeping the seam on top and completely encasing them.
2. Bake on a cookie sheet or jelly-roll pan in a preheated 400°F oven for 30 minutes, or until the potatoes are tender. Pinch the potatoes through the paper or foil with a hot-pad holder or an insulated glove to test for doneness.

Serves 6

Potato-Carrot Fritters

This unusual dish lifts the meal into a conversation piece, especially when served with broiled fresh fish.

5 medium-size potatoes (1¾ pounds), peeled and sliced
5 medium-size carrots, scraped and sliced
1½ cups flour
1 egg, lightly beaten
1½ teaspoons salt
½ teaspoon freshly ground pepper
⅛ teaspoon ground mace
⅓ cup milk
Vegetable oil

1. Cook the potatoes and carrots separately in salted water over medium heat until tender. Drain and dry over low heat in the same pan, reserving ⅓ cup of the cooking water from the carrots.
2. In a large bowl, mash together the potatoes and carrots, blending well. Using a wire whisk, whip in the flour, egg, salt, pepper, and mace. Gradually add the reserved carrot liquid. Beat in the milk.
3. Heat ¼ inch of vegetable oil in a large frying pan. Using a tablespoon, spoon out the potato-carrot mixture and carefully drop into the hot oil. Cook over medium heat, flipping the fritters to get them evenly browned. Drain on paper towels and serve immediately.

SERVES 6

Homemade Potato Chips

The story goes that one of the horsey set kept sending his fried potatoes back to the chef in a Saratoga, New York, restaurant, claiming they were soggy. Finally the chef became angry. He sliced the potatoes as thinly as he could and deep-fried them until they were so crisp that they broke when touched with a fork. The diner was delighted. Thus was born an American favorite, originally called Saratoga Chips.

The key to good chips is to slice the potatoes extremely thin, almost to the point of transparency. We use the thin slicer on the food processor, which is perfect. However, there are various kinds of slicers on the market that also do a good job.

6 medium-size baking potatoes (2 pounds), peeled and very thinly sliced
Vegetable oil for frying
Salt

1. Place the thinly sliced potatoes in a bowl of ice water for 1 hour. Drain. Dry well in a cloth.
2. Heat the oil to 350°F in a frying basket, mini-fryer, or skillet. (Add a few cubes of bread to hot oil—if they brown immediately, the oil is ready.) Add some of the potatoes. Do not overcrowd. Cook only one layer at a time. The potatoes must be completely immersed in the hot oil. Fry over medium, even heat until the potatoes are lightly brown and crisp. (Test fry a batch first, and sample the chips for crispness.)
3. Drain the potatoes on paper towels and sprinkle with salt.

Serves 6

Steak-Fried Potatoes

Steak fries are simple, easy to prepare, and make an excellent accompaniment to your favorite kind of steak.

The only technique involved here is patience. Remember, you are starting with raw potatoes. Don't try to rush the job, or the potatoes will not be cooked through.

We also like to vary these potatoes with another version called German Fries. Cook minced onions in some melted butter or margarine over medium heat until soft, then add preboiled potatoes, cut into ¼-inch-thick slices. Cook until the potatoes are evenly browned.

4 tablespoons (½ stick) butter or margarine
1 tablespoon olive oil
4 large potatoes (1¾ pounds), peeled and sliced ¼ inch thick.
Salt and freshly ground black pepper to taste

In a large frying pan, heat the butter or margarine and oil. Add the potatoes and cook evenly, turning often, until brown and crusty on the outside and soft and mealy inside, about 15 minutes. Season to taste with salt and pepper.

SERVES 4

Delhi Yogurt-Spiced Potatoes

Historians are still baffled about how the potato, discovered by the Spaniards in Peru and brought to Europe, managed to get to India. The Indians may have acquired them late, but they are way ahead in their many unique ways of cooking the vegetable. These potatoes are usually served chilled.

6 large potatoes (3 pounds)
2 tablespoons butter or margarine
1 tablespoon olive oil
1½ teaspoons cumin seeds
4 scallions, white part only, chopped
½ teaspoon hot Indian chili powder
Salt to taste
1½ cups low-fat yogurt

1. Boil the potatoes in their skins over medium heat until tender. Drain and dry over low heat in the same pan. Cool slightly, then peel and cut into ½-inch cubes.
2. In a deep saucepan, heat the butter or margarine and oil. Stir in the cumin seeds, cooking until the seeds crack and break. Stir in the scallions and chili powder. Add the potatoes.
3. Reduce the heat to low and, turning constantly, cook until the potatoes are coated. Remove from the heat.
4. Season to taste with salt and blend in the yogurt. Chill.

Serves 6 to 8

Diced Fries

Here's a quick, convenient way to fry potatoes. The addition of bread crumbs is a French touch.

4 tablespoons (½ stick) butter or margarine
1 teaspoon olive oil
4 medium-size potatoes (1¼ pounds), peeled and diced
Salt and freshly ground pepper to taste
3 tablespoons bread crumbs (optional)

1. Heat the butter or margarine and oil in a large frying pan. Add the potatoes, turning several times until well coated. Season with salt and pepper. Cook over low heat, turning occasionally with a spatula, until the potatoes are brown and tender.
2. If desired, sprinkle on the crumbs 5 minutes before serving.

SERVES 4

German Potato Fritters

3 large potatoes (1½ pounds)
2 cups chopped, cooked beef or lamb
1 small onion, minced
1 tablespoon butter or margarine
1 egg white, stiffly beaten
Salt and freshly ground pepper to taste
Vegetable oil

1. Cook the potatoes in their skins in boiling water over medium heat until tender. Drain. Dry over low heat in the same pan. Peel and mash.
2. Place the meat in a food processor or run through a meat grinder to chop finely.
3. Cook the onion in the butter or margarine until soft. Do not brown. Mix the onion with the potatoes and chopped meat in a large bowl. Add the egg white, salt, and pepper. Blend well. Form into 4 medium-thick patties.
4. Heat about ¼ inch oil in a frying pan. Cook the potato-meat patties quickly in the oil over medium-high heat until evenly browned on both sides.

SERVES 4

Potato-Stuffed Green Peppers

4 medium-size potatoes (about 1½ pounds)
6 large, firm green peppers
3 tablespoons butter or margarine
1 tablespoon vegetable oil
1 medium-size onion, finely chopped
½ teaspoon ground coriander
½ teaspoon mustard seed
½ teaspoon curry powder
Salt and freshly ground pepper to taste
2 teaspoons fresh lemon juice

1. Boil the potatoes in their skins over medium heat until almost tender. Drain and dry over low heat in the same pan. Peel and cut into ½-inch cubes.
2. Cut a slice off the top of the peppers. Trim the tops, finely chop, and set aside. Remove the seeds and white ribs from the pepper shells. Parboil the peppers in a large quantity of boiling water for 2 minutes. Invert, drain, and cool.
3. In a frying pan, heat 2 tablespoons of the butter or margarine and the oil. Add the onion and chopped pepper tops and cook for 3 minutes. Add the potatoes, and cook, turning often, until they are golden and tender, about 6 minutes. Just before the potatoes are completely cooked, stir in the coriander, mustard seed, curry powder, salt, and pepper.
4. Stuff the peppers with the potato mixture. Place in a baking dish just large enough to hold them, sprinkle with the lemon juice, and dot with the remaining 1 tablespoon of butter or margarine.
5. Pour about ¼ inch of water into the dish and bake, uncovered, in a preheated 350°F oven for 20 minutes, until the peppers are tender and heated through.

SERVES 6

Hungarian Potatoes with Mushrooms

7 medium-size potatoes (about 2¼ pounds), peeled
2 to 3 tablespoons butter or margarine
6 slices lean Canadian bacon
2 medium-size onions, finely chopped
½ pound fresh mushrooms, sliced
1 teaspoon Hungarian paprika
¾ cup low-fat sour cream
½ cup low-fat cottage cheese
Salt to taste
2 tablespoons chopped fresh parsley

1. Boil the potatoes in salted water over medium heat until tender. Drain and dry over low heat in the same pan. Cut into ½-inch cubes.
2. In a saucepan large enough to hold all the ingredients, heat 2 tablespoons butter or margarine and cook the bacon until crisp. Remove the bacon from the pan, dice, and set aside.
3. If the bacon has absorbed most of the butter or margarine, add 1 tablespoon more to the pan and cook the onions until soft. Do not brown. Add the mushrooms and cook for 2 minutes. Stir in the paprika, sour cream, cottage cheese, potatoes, and salt, and heat to a low simmer. Stir in the bacon pieces.
4. Transfer to a hot serving dish. Sprinkle with the parsley and serve.

SERVES 6

iced Potatoes with Yogurt

…edium-size potatoes (about 2 pounds)
⅛ teaspoon ground coriander
¼ teaspoon freshly ground black pepper
1 teaspoon ground cumin
¼ teaspoon ground cardamom
½ teaspoon red pepper flakes
2 tablespoons water
Salt to taste
1 tablespoon vegetable oil
2 tablespoons fresh lemon juice
¾ cup low-fat yogurt

1. Boil the potatoes in their skins, over medium heat, until tender. Drain and dry over low heat in the same pan. Peel and dice.
2. In a small bowl, combine the spices, water, and salt, blending well.
3. Heat the oil in a large frying pan, over medium heat. Add the potatoes, spice mixture, and the lemon juice. Cook, stirring, until well blended.
4. Remove the frying pan from the heat and stir in the yogurt. Taste for seasoning, adding more salt, if needed.

SERVES 4 TO 6

Potato Kreplach

You can serve this classic dish alone, with sour cream, or cooked in rich chicken broth and served as a main-dish soup, sprinkled with parsley.

Dough

2 cups all-purpose flour
2 eggs
1½ teaspoons salt
Warm water

Filling

4 medium-size potatoes (1¼ pounds)
2 small onions, minced
1 tablespoon butter or margarine
½ cup cottage cheese
1 egg yolk, beaten
1 tablespoon chopped fresh dill, or 1 teaspoon dried
Salt and freshly ground pepper to taste

½ cup (1 stick) butter or margarine

1. Mound the flour on a pastry board and make a well in the center. Break the eggs into the well, add the salt and 2 tablespoons of water. Mix thoroughly and knead into a smooth, firm dough. Add small amounts of water, if too firm, or more flour, if too soft.
2. Divide the dough into two parts and allow it to rest for ½ hour, covered with a bowl. While the dough is resting, make the filling.
3. Cook the potatoes in their skins in boiling water over medium heat until tender. Drain. Dry them over low heat in the same pan. Peel and mash.
4. In a frying pan, over medium heat, cook the onions in the butter or margarine until soft. Do not brown. Remove from the heat and cool slightly. Stir in the potatoes, cottage cheese, egg yolk, dill, salt, and pepper, blending well. Set aside.
5. Roll the dough on a floured board into ⅛-inch-thick, or thinner, sheets. Cut into 3-inch circles. Place a tablespoon of the filling just off center on each circle. Moisten the edges, fold over, and press the edges together to seal.

6. With a slotted spoon, lower the kreplach into gently boiling water, and cook, covered, until they rise to the top, about 7 minutes.
7. Remove with a slotted spoon and drain. Either brown the kreplach in butter or margarine or serve drizzled with melted butter or margarine.

Makes about 25

Lemon Dill Potatoes

24 small new potatoes (about 3 pounds)
3 tablespoons butter or margarine
3 tablespoons flour
½ cup milk
½ cup half-and-half
2 tablespoons fresh lemon juice
Salt and freshly ground pepper to taste
2 tablespoons chopped fresh dill

1. Boil the potatoes in their skins until tender. Drain. Dry over low heat in the same pan.
2. While the potatoes are cooking, make the sauce. In a saucepan, over medium heat, melt the butter or margarine. Add the flour and cook, stirring, until you have a smooth paste. Gradually add the milk and half-and-half, stirring constantly, until the sauce is smooth and thick. Stir in the lemon juice, salt, and pepper.
3. Peel the potatoes while they are still warm. Pour the hot sauce over them, and sprinkle with fresh dill.

Serves 6

Maine Potato Dumplings

These are good served with a meat stew, the gravy spooned over the dumplings.

1 cup leftover mashed potatoes
1 cup all-purpose flour
1½ teaspoons salt
3 egg yolks, beaten

1. In a bowl, mix together all the ingredients. Using a tablespoon, shape the mixture into balls. With a slotted spoon, lower the balls into gently boiling, salted water. Cook for 10 minutes.
2. Remove the dumplings with the slotted spoon and drain.

SERVES 2

Potatoes Madeira

We first enjoyed this dish on the Portuguese island of Madeira, where it was served with fresh mackerel cooked in a spicy tomato sauce. The flavor and the scent of the potatoes are unique. It won't taste the same if you use dried oregano.

8 medium-small new potatoes (about 1¼ pounds)
1 large bunch fresh oregano, washed and dried
Salt and freshly ground pepper to taste
4 tablespoons (½ stick) butter or margarine, melted

1. Put the potatoes and fresh oregano in a large pot. Cover with water. Bring to a boil over medium heat and cook until tender. Discard the oregano.
2. Drain the potatoes and dry over low heat in the same pan.
3. Serve the potatoes in their skins, split. Season with salt and pepper and drizzle with melted butter or margarine.

SERVES 4

Potato and Mushroom Bake

½ pound fresh mushrooms, sliced
1 tablespoon of flour
6 medium-size potatoes (about 2 pounds), peeled and cut into ⅛-inch-thick slices
2 small white onions, finely chopped
3 tablespoons finely chopped fresh parsley
1 cup grated Swiss cheese
Salt and freshly ground pepper to taste
¾ cup half-and-half
¾ cup milk
2 tablespoons butter or margarine

1. Butter a shallow baking dish. Toss the mushrooms with the flour. In the dish, arrange a layer of potato slices, a layer of mushrooms, then a sprinkling of onions. Top the onions with some of the parsley and cheese, salt, and pep-

per. Repeat the layers, reserving ¼ cup cheese and finishing with potatoes.

2. Mix the half-and-half and milk and pour over the layers. Sprinkle with the remaining ¼ cup cheese and dot with the butter or margarine.

3. Bake in a preheated 325°F oven for 45 minutes, or until the potatoes are tender and the top is golden. If the top starts getting too brown before the potatoes are cooked, cover dish loosely with foil.

SERVES 4 TO 6

New Potatoes, Swiss Chard, and Chick-peas

16 tiny new potatoes (about 1¾ pounds), scrubbed
¾ pound Swiss chard, washed, drained, middle rib removed, and coarsely chopped
1 cup Chicken Broth (page 22), or canned
1 medium-size onion, chopped
1 garlic clove, minced
2 tablespoons butter or margarine
3 large, ripe tomatoes, peeled, seeded, and chopped
⅛ teaspoon red pepper flakes
⅛ teaspoon dried oregano
1 teaspoon sugar
Salt to taste
1 cup rinsed, drained, and cooked canned chick-peas
½ cup grated Asiago or Parmesan cheese

1. Boil the potatoes in their skins over medium heat until tender. Drain and dry over low heat in the same pot.

2. Remove the potatoes and set aside. In the same pot, over medium heat, cook the Swiss chard in the chicken broth until tender. Drain, saving the broth and reserving the chard.
3. In a large frying pan, cook the onion and garlic in the butter or margarine for about 2 minutes, or until softened. Do not brown. Add the reserved broth, the tomatoes, pepper flakes, oregano, sugar, and salt. Simmer, uncovered, for 15 minutes, or until the sauce thickens.
4. Meanwhile, remove a band of skin from the center third of the potatoes, leaving skin on both ends. Stir the potatoes, chard, and chick-peas into the sauce. Simmer 5 minutes, or until heated through. Serve with the grated cheese at the table.

Serves 4

Paprika-Cream Potatoes

1 cup low-fat sour cream
¼ cup half-and-half
1 teaspoon Hungarian paprika
3 tablespoons butter or margarine
2 tablespoons vegetable oil
6 medium-size potatoes (about 2 pounds), peeled and cut into ½-inch cubes
2 scallions, white part and some light green, trimmed and finely chopped
Salt to taste

1. In a small bowl, blend together the sour cream, half-and-half, and paprika. Set aside.

2. In a large frying pan, heat the butter or margarine and oil. Add the potatoes and cook, covered, for 20 minutes, or until tender and golden. Shake the pan often to prevent the potatoes from sticking.
3. Stir in the scallions and salt. Cook for 1 minute.
4. Carefully blend in the sour cream mixture. Heat to a simmer and serve.

SERVES 4 TO 6

Parmesan Potatoes

The Italians bring their unique culinary imagination and flavoring techniques to the *patata,* a food that they value next only to pasta.

They like to serve these potatoes with tender young roast lamb, delicately flavored with rosemary.

6 medium-size potatoes (about 2 pounds)
3 tablespoons butter or margarine
1 tablespoon olive oil
1½ teaspoons finely crumbled dry leaf sage
1 cup (4 ounces) grated Parmesan cheese
Salt to taste
⅛ teaspoon red pepper flakes

1. Peel the potatoes and cut into wedges. Cook the potatoes over medium heat in boiling salted water until tender but still slightly firm *(al dente).* Drain. Dry potatoes over low heat in the same pan. Set aside and keep warm.
2. In a large frying pan, heat the butter or margarine and oil. Stir in the sage and cook over medium heat until the butter or margarine is light brown. Add the potatoes, Par-

mesan, salt, and pepper flakes, turning the potatoes several times until they are well coated and heated through.

Serves 6

Potatoes with Small Pasta Shells

3 tablespoons olive oil
1 large onion, coarsely chopped
1 garlic clove, minced
6 medium-size potatoes (2 pounds), peeled and cut into ¾-inch cubes
One 28-ounce can tomatoes
⅛ teaspoon ground cinnamon
½ teaspoon dried basil
Salt and freshly ground pepper to taste
½ pound small pasta shells (maruzzini)
2 tablespoons chopped fresh broadleaf parsley
½ cup grated Asiago or Parmesan cheese

1. In a large saucepan, heat the oil. Add the onion and garlic and cook until the onion is transparent. Add the potatoes and cook for 10 minutes, stirring.
2. Place the tomatoes in a bowl and break them up. Add the tomatoes, cinnamon, basil, salt, and pepper to the potato pan. Simmer, uncovered, for 20 minutes, or until the sauce thickens and the potatoes are tender. If the sauce thickens before the potatoes are done, cover the pan.
3. Meanwhile, cook the pasta shells in gently boiling salted water. Drain well and add to the potato-tomato mixture. Simmer for 5 minutes. Stir in the parsley and serve, passing the cheese at the table.

Serves 6 to 8

German Sour Potatoes

7 medium-size potatoes (2¼ pounds)
4 slices lean bacon, cut into ¼-inch squares
1 large onion, chopped
3 tablespoons flour
½ teaspoon celery salt
Pinch of dried thyme
Freshly ground pepper to taste
2½ cups beef broth
3 tablespoons white vinegar
Salt to taste
2 tablespoons chopped fresh parsley

1. Peel the potatoes and boil in salted water over medium heat until tender. Do not overcook. Drain and dry over low heat in the same pan. Cut into ¼-inch-thick slices. Set aside.
2. In a saucepan, over medium heat, sauté the bacon until golden. Add the onion and cook until transparent. Stir in the flour and cook over low heat, stirring constantly, until the flour is golden. Season with celery salt, thyme, and pepper.
3. Slowly stir in the beef broth and cook, stirring, until the sauce is smooth and thick. Add the vinegar and simmer, covered, for 7 minutes. If the sauce is too thick, add more broth. Taste for seasoning.
4. Add the potatoes to the sauce and mix well but carefully. Heat to a simmer. Sprinkle with the parsley and serve.

SERVES 6

Swedish Anchovy Potatoes

6 medium-size potatoes (2 pounds), peeled and cut into long, thin strips
3 medium-size white onions, thinly sliced
Two 2-ounce cans of flat anchovy fillets, drained
½ teaspoon freshly ground pepper
¾ cup half-and-half
¾ cup milk
2 tablespoons unsalted butter or margarine

1. In a lightly buttered baking dish, arrange a layer of potato strips, then onions. Lay half the anchovies over the onions and sprinkle with pepper. Repeat, ending with a layer of potatoes.
2. Mix together the half-and-half and milk, then pour 1 cup over the layers. Dot with butter or margarine.
3. Bake, uncovered, in a preheated 375°F oven for 35 minutes. Add the remaining ½ cup milk mixture and cook for 10 minutes longer, or until the casserole bubbles and the potatoes are tender. If the top gets brown before the potatoes are tender, cover the dish lightly with foil.

SERVES 4 TO 6

Turkish Potato Balls

6 medium-size potatoes (2 pounds)
3 tablespoons butter or margarine
2 tablespoons low-fat yogurt
¼ teaspoon dried oregano
½ teaspoon seasoned salt

⅛ teaspoon cayenne
1 tablespoon flour
2 tablespoons toasted bread crumbs
1 whole egg and 1 egg yolk, beaten together
1 egg, beaten, for dipping
Bread crumbs for dredging
Vegetable oil for deep-frying

1. Boil the potatoes in their skins over medium heat until tender. Drain and dry over low heat in the same pan. Peel.
2. In a large bowl, mash the hot potatoes with the butter or margarine, yogurt, oregano, seasoned salt, cayenne, flour, and toasted bread crumbs. Taste for seasoning. When mixture is slightly cooled, beat in the egg and yolk.
3. Flour your hands and shape the mixture into Ping-Pong-size balls. Dip the balls in the beaten egg, then dredge with bread crumbs. Deep-fry in the vegetable oil, a few at a time until golden. Do not crowd.
4. Drain the balls on paper towels. Keep warm in a 250°F oven while cooking the remaining balls. Serve while still crisp.

SERVES 4 TO 6

Potato–Turnip Custard

3 large potatoes (about 1¼ pounds), peeled and diced
1 pound turnips, peeled and diced
3 eggs
1½ cups hot milk
2 tablespoons butter or margarine, melted
2 tablespoons grated onion
Salt and freshly ground pepper to taste

1. Boil the potatoes and turnips separately in salted water over medium heat. Drain and dry both vegetables over low heat in the same cooking pan. Mash each separately and then mix together. Cool slightly.
2. In a large bowl, beat the eggs. Blend in the mashed potatoes and turnips, the milk, butter or margarine, onion, salt, and pepper. Pour mixture into a shallow baking dish. Set in a pan of hot water (the water should come halfway up the side of the dish).
3. Bake in a preheated 350°F oven for 30 minutes, or until set. Do not overcook.

Serves 4 to 6

Potatoes in Vegetable Sauce

4 tablespoons (½ stick) butter or margarine
2 tablespoons olive oil
4 large potatoes (1¾ pounds), peeled and cut into ½-inch cubes
Salt and freshly ground pepper to taste
1 small onion, chopped
1 garlic clove, minced
1 small green pepper, seeded, cored, and cut into thin strips
2 medium-size, ripe tomatoes, peeled, seeded, and diced
½ teaspoon sugar
½ cup cut-up fresh green beans
1 small zucchini, cubed (about 1 cup)
1 teaspoon chili powder

1. Heat 2 tablespoons butter or margarine and the oil in a frying pan. Add the potatoes and cook, turning occasion-

ally, until tender and golden. Season with salt and pepper. Set aside and keep warm.

2. In a saucepan, melt the remaining 2 tablespoons butter or margarine. Over medium heat, add the onion, garlic, and green pepper and cook for 2 minutes. Add the tomatoes, sugar, and green beans. Cook another 10 minutes, or until the beans are tender but still crunchy and the sauce thickens.

3. Stir the zucchini, chili powder, and salt and pepper to taste into the sauce. Cook until the zucchini is crunchy tender. Taste for seasoning.

4. Transfer the hot potatoes to a warm serving dish. Spoon over the vegetable sauce.

SERVES 4 TO 6

Potatoes "Vol-au-Vent"

Excellent served with an omelet or broiled fish.

6 uniform long baking potatoes (2½ pounds), peeled
6 tablespoons (¾ stick) butter or margarine
2 tablespoons olive oil
¼ cup chopped shallots
6 medium-size fresh mushrooms, coarsely chopped
2 tablespoons flour
Pinch of cayenne
½ cup half-and-half
½ cup milk
1 cup coarsely chopped Canadian bacon
Salt to taste
¼ cup grated cheese

1. Using a melon ball cutter, scoop out part of the insides of the potatoes lengthwise, leaving a good ½-inch-thick shell. Discard the scooped-out portion or use in another recipe. Over medium heat, cook the potato shells in boiling salted water for 10 minutes. Drain. Dry out the potato shells in the same pan over low heat.
2. Melt 3 tablespoons butter or margarine and combine with the olive oil, then rub the outside of the potato shells with the mixture. Bake in an uncovered pan, hollow-side down, in a preheated 425°F oven for 20 minutes. The potatoes should be golden and tender when pricked with the point of a knife.
3. While the potatoes are baking, make the filling. In a frying pan, melt 3 tablespoons of butter or margarine. Add the shallots and cook for 3 minutes, or until soft. Do not brown. Add the mushrooms and cook 3 minutes. Sprinkle in the flour and cayenne and mix well. Blend together the half-and-half and milk and slowly stir into the filling mixture. Cook until the sauce thickens. Stir in the bacon. Taste for seasoning, adding salt, if necessary.
4. Fill the baked potato shells with the mushroom-bacon filling. Sprinkle the top with grated cheese and lightly brown under the broiler.

Serves 6

7

Bakers and Pancakes

BAKERS

Many restaurants and fast-food places, monuments to the appeal and versatility of our favorite vegetable, feature the baked potato as the main attraction.

Franchised specialty potato restaurants are having a successful run in California and elsewhere in the country, serving baked potatoes with various tempting toppings ranging from avocado and cheese to rare steak and seafood and chicken combinations.

A waiter serves you a huge Idaho potato, baked to perfection and wrapped snugly in foil to keep it piping hot. The potato is split and neatly spread with the topping of your choice. There it is, two meals in one: a nice tender piece of pink steak and underneath the mealy, buttery, moist baked potato.

Baked potato restaurants also are starting up in Europe. The Scandinavians offer baked potato halves mixed with various fish and shellfish. Their tiny tender shrimp topped with butter and a sprinkling of fresh dill are superb on top of a baked potato.

So far as baked potatoes are concerned, just about anything goes. It's fun and rewarding to experiment.

We've found that scooping out the baked potato pulp, mashing it with butter or margarine, blending in finely chopped, garden-fresh scallions, and then returning it to the shell and heating it for a few minutes is a unique, zesty way to fix a baked potato.

Another potato treat is a baked potato filled with a creamy mashed potato filling and topped with caviar.

HOW TO BAKE A POTATO

Baking is probably the oldest method of cooking a potato. Today it pays to use Idahoes, although Long Island Russets and Main Kennebecs are also superb. For even cooking, buy block-shaped potatoes that have no pronounced taper.

Wash the potatoes well, dry, and pierce the skin. Piercing or making a small incision in the skin in several places allows the steam to escape and also prevents the potato from bursting. Some cooks like to rub the skin with oil to give it a shiny, soft texture. (The skin of the potato is good for you and delicious, too.) Others use foil to keep the potato hot longer.

A medium-size potato (three per pound) bakes in about 1 hour at 400°F. Place the potatoes on an oven rack or a baking sheet. Never bake them on the bottom of the oven itself, for that will produce potatoes that are too soft. To make sure the potato is done, pinch it. If it is soft, it's cooked. Potatoes also cook well and fast in a microwave oven. Check your instruction booklet for exact directions or see pages 17–19.

Remember, too, that leftover baked potatoes come in handy for future recipes. In fact, bake a few extra ones and have them later mashed, as hash browns, minced in cream, or au gratin.

The following innovative toppings make new and interesting potato side dishes or even entrées.

For those who haven't the time or the inclination to experiment making their own baked potato combinations, a number of complete baked potato recipes follow. Many make excellent luncheon or supper dishes.

Aunt Edie's Roasted Potatoes

Another good recipe from our friend Barbara M. Valbona.

4 large baking potatoes (about 2¼ pounds), scrubbed
2 garlic cloves, minced
3 tablespoons vegetable oil
Salt and freshly ground pepper to taste
1 tablespoon dried oregano
1½ tablespoons paprika

1. Dry the potatoes, then cut into eighths lengthwise.
2. Place the potato pieces in a casserole. Sprinkle with the remaining ingredients. With your hands, mix all the ingredients until the potatoes are thoroughly coated.
3. Bake the potatoes in a preheated 400°F oven for 1 hour, or until the potatoes can be pierced easily with a fork.

SERVES 6

BAKED POTATO TOPPINGS

Salt and freshly ground coarse black pepper
Seasoned salt, seasoned pepper
Snipped parsley, dill, watercress, or chives
Chopped drained pimiento
Low-calorie salad dressing
Low-fat shredded cheese with thinly sliced sweet Spanish onions or scallions
Whipped butter or margarine
Lemon butter or margarine
Hot skim milk or chicken broth seasoned with herbs
Low-fat sour cream
Low-fat yogurt
Cottage cheese combined with chives, dill, pimiento, or tomatoes
Marinated mushrooms
Mock sour cream (cottage cheese whipped in a blender)
Roquefort cheese

Bacon-Stuffed Potatoes

4 large baking potatoes (2¼ pounds), scrubbed
4 slices of lean Canadian bacon, each rolled tightly
Melted butter or margarine
Salt

1. Bake the potatoes for 35 minutes in a preheated 400°F oven. Using an oven mitt to hold the potato, hollow out a tubular opening in one end of each potato, large enough

Baked Potato Toppings (*Continued*)
Avocado mashed with low-fat sour cream
Whipped cream cheese with chives
Cheese sauce
Diced ham and cheese
Clam chowder
Shrimp creole
"Sloppy Joe"–style tomato and meat sauce
Creamed or curried chicken
Chopped beef and onion, or creamed chipped beef
Sausage meat and scallions
Chili sauce
Sliced sausages or frankfurters
Nuggets of Gorgonzola cheese
Sauerkraut and strips of corned beef
Chopped ham and egg, bacon and egg, or crisp bacon bits
Lamb, beef, or chicken stew, canned or homemade
Turkey and cheese sauce
Parmesan cheese, blended with butter or margarine, garlic, or parsley
Cheddar cheese and fresh tomato

to accommodate a bacon roll. Reserve the end pieces removed from the potato.

2. Insert the bacon roll into each opening. Replace the potato end pieces.

3. Place the stuffed potatoes on a baking sheet. Return to the oven and cook until the potatoes are soft, about 15 minutes longer.

4. Cut the potatoes halfway through and serve with the melted butter or margarine and salt.

SERVES 4

❧

Potatoes à la Boursin

This recipe comes from the French Boursin cheese country.

4 medium-size baking potatoes (1½ pounds), scrubbed
4 tablespoons soft herb and garlic cheese

1. Bake the potatoes in 400°F oven for 1 hour, or until soft.
2. Cook, then cut the potatoes in half lengthwise. With a fork, carefully mash the potatoes in the skins. Press 1 tablespoonful of herb and garlic cheese into one half of each potato. Replace the other half potato, pressing them together, thus "sandwiching" the cheese between the halves.
3. Wrap each potato in foil and bake in a preheated 400°F oven for 15 minutes, or until heated through.

Serves 4

Crab-Stuffed Baked Potatoes

Here's a tasty, fast main-dish potato surprise.

4 medium-size baking potatoes (1½ pounds), scrubbed
2 tablespoons grated onion
¼ cup milk
One 10-ounce can shrimp bisque soup
⅛ teaspoon cayenne
½ cup grated Cheddar cheese

One 7-ounce can crabmeat, cleaned and flaked
Salt to taste

1. Bake the potatoes in a 400°F oven for 1 hour, or until soft.
2. In a saucepan, combine the onion, milk, shrimp bisque, and cayenne. Cook over low heat, stirring, for 6 minutes. Add the cheese, stirring until it melts. Stir in the crabmeat. Set aside.
3. Split the potatoes lengthwise and scoop out all of the pulp, reserving the 4 best shells. Rice the pulp into a bowl and gradually mix in half the soup-cheese-crabmeat sauce. Taste for seasoning. Spoon the mixture into the 4 potato shells.
4. Place the stuffed shells on a baking sheet. Spoon over the remaining seafood sauce and bake in a preheated 450°F oven for 10 minutes, or until heated through.

SERVES 4

Baked Potatoes Stuffed with Creamed Cabbage

6 medium-size baking potatoes (2 pounds), scrubbed
5 tablespoons butter or margarine
3 cups finely shredded, tender green cabbage
1 garlic clove, minced
½ teaspoon caraway seeds
Salt and freshly ground pepper to taste
2 teaspoons fresh lemon juice
½ teaspoon brown sugar
½ cup low-fat sour cream

1. Bake the potatoes in a 400°F oven for 1 hour, or until soft.
2. While the potatoes are baking, prepare the creamed cabbage. In a frying pan, melt 2 tablespoons butter or margarine. Stir in the cabbage, garlic, caraway seeds, salt, and pepper. Cover tightly. Over medium-low heat, steam until the cabbage is tender and the liquid has evaporated. Stir in the lemon juice, brown sugar, and sour cream. Heat through but do not boil.
3. Cut a thin slice lengthwise from the top of each potato. Scoop out the pulp, reserving the large bottom shells, and mash with the remaining 3 tablespoons butter or margarine. Season with salt and pepper.
4. Return the mashed pulp to the potato shells. Place the shells on a baking sheet and spoon the cabbage mixture onto the mashed potatoes.
5. Bake in a preheated 400°F oven for 15 minutes, or until heated through.

Serves 6

Easy New England Chowdered Potatoes

6 medium to large baking potatoes (2 to 3 pounds), scrubbed
4 tablespoons (½ stick) butter or margarine
Two 6½-ounce cans minced clams, drained
½ teaspoon salt
Paprika
One 15-ounce can New England clam chowder

1. Bake the potatoes in a 400°F oven for 1 hour, or until soft.
2. Cut a large X lengthwise in the skin of each potato. Fold back the skin and remove the pulp. Reserve the shells.
3. In a bowl, mash the pulp with the butter or margarine. Add the clams and salt and blend well. Taste for seasoning. Spoon the mixture back into the potato shells. Sprinkle with paprika.
4. Bake the stuffed shells on a baking sheet in a preheated 400°F oven for 15 minutes, or until heated through and golden on top.
5. Meanwhile, heat the soup according to label directions. Serve the soup in a sauceboat as a topping for the potatoes.

SERVES 6

Baked French-Fried Slices

4 medium-size baking potatoes (1½ pounds), scrubbed
Vegetable oil for deep-frying
Salt and freshly ground pepper to taste

1. Bake the potatoes for 1 hour in a 400°F oven, or until soft.
2. While the potatoes are in the last stage of baking (still somewhat firm), heat 2 inches of oil until a cube of bread sizzles and browns quickly when dropped into it. Keep the oil at that heat.
3. Remove the potatoes from the oven and cut into ⅓-inch-thick slices. Do not peel. Fry the slices quickly, just until they are crusted and golden. Drain on paper towels and season with salt and pepper. Serve immediately.

SERVES 4

Shrimp–Stuffed Potatoes

6 medium-size baking potatoes (about 2 pounds), scrubbed
12 medium-size cooked shrimp, coarsely chopped
5 tablespoons butter or margarine
⅓ cup grated Parmesan cheese
Salt and freshly ground pepper to taste

1. Bake the potatoes in a 400°F oven for 1 hour, or until soft.
2. Cut the potatoes lengthwise and remove the pulp, reserving the 6 best shells. Rice the pulp into a bowl. Add the shrimp, butter or margarine, half the Parmesan, the salt, and pepper. Blend thoroughly.
3. Spoon the mixture back into the 6 reserved shells and bake in a preheated 375°F oven on a baking sheet, until the top starts to turn golden, about 15 minutes.

Serves 6

Baked New Potato Surprise

New potatoes are not usually baked, but here's a surprisingly delicious exception. We like to surround a standing rib roast with these delicious morsels.

24 small new potatoes (about 2 pounds), washed and dried
Olive oil
2 teaspoons salt

1. Rub the potatoes with olive oil, cut them in half, and sprinkle with salt.
2. Arrange on a baking sheet and bake in a preheated 450°F oven for 40 minutes, or until the potatoes are tender, puffed, and browned.

SERVES 6

Baked Potatoes Stuffed with Oysters

Here's elegance in a potato skin!

6 large baking potatoes (about 3 pounds), scrubbed
5 tablespoons butter or margarine
1 tablespoon minced shallots
¼ pound mushrooms, coarsely chopped
1½ tablespoons flour
Salt to taste
1 cup milk
1 teaspoon Worcestershire sauce
Pinch of cayenne
12 fresh small shucked oysters
3 tablespoons grated cheese

1. Bake the potatoes in a 400°F oven for 1 hour, or until soft.
2. While the potatoes are baking, prepare the stuffing. In a frying pan, heat 2 tablespoons butter or margarine. Add the shallots and cook for 1 minute, or until soft. Do not brown. Add the mushrooms and cook 1 minute longer. Sprinkle in the flour and salt and cook, stirring constantly. Gradually stir in the milk, Worcestershire sauce, and cayenne. Cook, stirring, until the sauce is medium thick and smooth.

3. When the potatoes are cooked, cut a thin slice from the top, lengthwise. Scoop out the pulp, reserving the shells, and mash the pulp with the remaining 3 tablespoons butter or margarine. Salt to taste. Spoon two-thirds of the potato pulp back into the shells. (Use the remainder in another recipe.)
4. Add the oysters to the mushroom sauce and simmer until the edges curl and the oysters become plump.
5. Place the potatoes in a baking dish. Spoon the mushroom-oyster sauce onto the potatoes in the shells. Sprinkle cheese on top and place in a preheated 425°F oven for 10 minutes, or until top is golden and potatoes are heated through.

Serves 6

POTATO PANCAKES

The versatile potato not only makes an excellent side dish and a delicious and satisfying main meal, but is a star when it comes to breakfast, brunch, and late-night suppers. One of the most unusual and international of its many forms is the pancake.

Here we offer many versions of potato "cakes" of one sort or another—from Ireland, Germany, India, Denmark, Russia, France, and the U.S.A. They're easy to prepare, make economical meals, and please everyone.

All Saints' Day Pancake

In Ireland, this dish is served on the eve of All Saints' Day.

8 medium-size baking potatoes (about 2¾ pounds), peeled, grated, and squeezed dry in a kitchen towel
1¼ cups flour
1½ teaspoons salt
½ cup milk
7 tablespoons butter or margarine
¼ cup firmly packed light brown sugar

1. In a large bowl, combine the potatoes, flour, and salt. Gradually add the milk, blending until the mixture holds together. Set aside for 45 minutes.
2. In a frying pan large enough to accommodate the mixture, melt 4 tablespoons butter or margarine. Add the potato mixture, shaping it with a spatula into a large thick cake. Cook over medium-low heat for 20 minutes, or until the underside is crusty brown. Use the spatula to keep the pancake from sticking to the bottom of the pan. Turn and cook until the entire pancake is browned.
3. Melt the remaining butter or margarine, and serve sprinkled over the pancake along with the brown sugar.

SERVES 6

Beefed-up Pancakes

8 medium-size baking potatoes (about 3 pounds), peeled and grated into a bowl of cold water
1 cup cold beef broth
2 eggs
1 cup flour, approximately
1½ teaspoons salt
½ teaspoon freshly ground pepper

1. Soak the potatoes in the water for 10 minutes. Drain and squeeze dry in a kitchen towel.
2. In a bowl, combine the potatoes, broth, eggs, ½ cup flour, salt, and pepper. Beat well. The batter should approximate that of ordinary pancake batter. If the batter is too thin, add small amounts of the remaining flour until the batter is of the proper consistency.
3. Grease a pancake griddle and spoon on enough of the batter to make medium-size cakes. Cook until crisply golden brown on both sides.

Serves 6

German Pancakes

4 large baking potatoes (2¼ pounds), peeled
2 medium-size potatoes, boiled and mashed (about 1⅓ cups)
2 eggs, beaten
1½ teaspoons salt
¼ cup milk

1. Grate the raw potatoes into a bowl half filled with water. Remove the potatoes. Pour the liquid from the bowl, but retain any starchy residue that has collected in the bottom. Squeeze the moisture from the potatoes in a kitchen towel.
2. In a large bowl, combine the grated potatoes, mashed potatoes, and the potato starch from the bottom of the bowl. Add the eggs, salt, and milk. Vigorously beat into a batter.
3. Put the batter, a tablespoonful at a time, on a greased hot griddle. Do not crowd. Cook until golden brown on both sides, turning once. Drain on paper towels. Serve immediately.

SERVES 4 TO 6

Bombay Potato Cakes

5 medium-size potatoes (about 1¾ pounds)
1 tablespoon butter or margarine, softened
1 teaspoon salt
¼ teaspoon cayenne, or to taste
½ teaspoon ground turmeric
7 tablespoons rice flour, or more
Vegetable oil for deep-frying

1. Peel the potatoes and cook in boiling, salted water over medium heat until tender. Drain. Dry over low heat in the same pan, then mash.
2. In a large bowl, combine the potatoes, butter or margarine, salt, cayenne, turmeric, and the rice flour. Mix well. The mixture should hold together as a firm dough; add more rice flour, if necessary.

3. Heat at least 2 inches of oil in a deep-fryer or pan. Pinch off balls of dough that, when flattened, make 2-inch cakes. When the oil is hot enough to brown a bread cube quickly, slide the cakes into the pan, one at a time, cooking several at once without crowding.
4. Fry the cakes for 2 minutes, or until golden brown and slightly crusty on both sides. Remove with slotted spatula and drain on paper towels. Serve immediately.

Serves 4

Copenhagen Cakes

These small Danish potato cakes are sometimes served with fruit preserves or maple syrup, but they most often accompany roast meat. They are rather soft cakes with a different and delightful flavor.

1 egg
1 cup milk
½ cup flour
2 tablespoons butter or margarine, melted
1 teaspoon salt
½ teaspoon freshly ground pepper
4 medium-size baking potatoes (1½ pounds), peeled and cubed
Vegetable oil

1. Combine the egg, milk, flour, butter or margarine, salt, and pepper in a blender jar. Blend on high for 30 seconds. Gradually add the potato cubes and blend again until mixture makes a thick smooth batter.

2. Lightly coat a frying pan with oil. Over medium heat cook the cakes, using 1 tablespoonful batter for each cake. Fry until golden brown on both sides.

SERVES 4

French Pancakes

½ cup light cream
2 tablespoons butter or margarine, melted
1 tablespoon olive oil
2 tablespoons beer
2 eggs
1 cup flour
1½ teaspoons salt
½ teaspoon freshly ground pepper
⅛ teaspoon cayenne
5 medium-size baking potatoes (1¾ pounds), peeled and finely shredded
Vegetable oil for frying

1. In a large bowl, mix together the cream, butter or margarine, olive oil, beer, eggs, flour, salt, pepper, and cayenne. Beat until well blended, then strain the batter into another large bowl, to make sure it's free from lumps.
2. Mix the shredded potatoes with the batter.
3. Heat about ¼ inch oil in a deep-frying pan. When the oil sizzles, add the batter by the tablespoonful to the pan. Cook the pancakes until golden brown on both sides.

SERVES 4 TO 6

d-fashioned American Potato Pancakes

Bacon fat is part of the classic potato pancake tradition, but use vegetable oil, if you prefer.

5 large baking potatoes (about 2¾ pounds), peeled and finely grated
½ large onion, grated
1 tablespoon flour
1 egg, lightly beaten
1 teaspoon salt
Freshly ground pepper to taste
About ¼ cup bacon fat or vegetable oil

1. In a large bowl, combine all the ingredients, except the bacon fat or oil. Blend well.
2. In a heavy-bottomed frying pan, melt 1 tablespoon bacon fat over medium heat, or add the oil. Cook 3 or 4 pancakes at a time, using a heaping tablespoonful of batter for each pancake. Press each one down with a spatula. If desired, use two frying pans in order to cook the pancakes quickly. Cook until they are brown on both sides, with lacy-crisp edges.

MAKES 12 PANCAKES

Potato Latkes

JEWISH POTATO PANCAKES

Serve with meat dishes, applesauce on the side.

4 large baking potatoes (2¼ pounds), peeled, grated, and squeezed dry in a kitchen towel
1 large white onion, grated
2 eggs, beaten
3 tablespoons matzo flour (available in supermarkets)
½ teaspoon baking powder
1½ teaspoons salt
½ teaspoon freshly ground pepper
½ cup vegetable oil

1. In a large bowl, blend the potatoes and onion. Stir in the eggs. Add the matzo flour, baking powder, salt, and pepper. Mix thoroughly.
2. In a frying pan, heat the oil until hot. Drop the potato mixture in by the tablespoonful. Press into cakes with a spatula and cook until golden brown and crusty on both sides. Add more oil if needed. Drain on paper towels.

MAKES ABOUT 12 PANCAKES, TO SERVE 4 TO 6

Easy Potato Pancakes

2 eggs, separated
2 tablespoons flour
1½ teaspoons salt
½ teaspoon freshly ground pepper
8 medium-size baking potatoes (about 2½ pounds), peeled
Vegetable oil for frying

1. In a large bowl, beat together the egg yolks, flour, salt, and pepper. Set aside.
2. Grate the potatoes as quickly as possible into a strainer, over a bowl. With the back of a spoon, press as much liquid out of the potatoes as possible. Pour off liquid that collected in the bowl, but reserve any starchy residue that remains in the bottom.
3. Blend the grated potatoes with the egg yolk mixture, then add the starchy residue. Beat the egg whites until stiff, then fold them in.
4. In a deep-frying pan, heat ½ cup oil. Place 1 heaping tablespoonful of the potato mixture in the pan for each cake. Press down with a spatula. Fry until golden brown and crispy on each side, turning once. Drain on paper towels. Serve immediately.

SERVES 6

Rhinelander Potato-Onion Cakes

In some sections of Germany potato pancakes are served with slices or bits of crisp bacon. Some German recipes also insist that potato pancakes should be cooked in bacon fat, although that's not absolutely necessary. It does make a difference in the taste, however.

Some other variations: Omit the onion and substitute 1 large peeled and chopped apple. Or add 2 tablespoons chopped broadleaf parsley to the batter.

3 small onions, finely chopped
2 eggs, beaten
½ cup flour
Salt
½ teaspoon freshly ground pepper
1½ cups milk
6 medium-size baking potatoes (2 pounds), peeled
Vegetable oil for frying

1. Blend the onions, eggs, flour, 1½ teaspoons salt, and pepper into a large bowl. Set aside.
2. Place the milk in a large bowl and grate the potatoes into the milk. Drain well, and discard the milk. Add the potatoes to the onion mixture. Mix thoroughly.
3. Heat ½ cup oil in a deep-frying pan. Over medium-high heat, drop the batter in by the tablespoonful to make the size cake desired. Add more oil as needed. As the batter cooks and takes shape, form it into cakes, using a spatula, and brown on both sides until crisp. Drain on paper towels.
4. Sprinkle lightly with salt and serve immediately.

SERVES 4

❧

ussian Potato Cakes

¼ cup warm water
1 package dry yeast
1 teaspoon sugar
1 teaspoon salt
½ cup flour
1 egg, beaten
6 medium-size baking potatoes (2 pounds), peeled, grated, and squeezed dry in a kitchen towel
Low-fat sour cream or yogurt

1. Blend warm water, yeast, sugar, salt, and flour in a large bowl.
2. Add the egg and potatoes to the bowl, and blend well. Set the dough aside to rise in a warm place for 10 minutes.
3. Over medium-high heat, drop rounded portions of dough onto a greased pancake griddle, forming cakes of whatever size you prefer. Cook until golden brown on both sides, turning once.
4. Serve with the sour cream or yogurt on the side.

Serves 4 to 6

8

Classic Potato Dishes

HERE ARE THOSE CLASSIC POTATO RECIPES THAT THROUGH TIME and tradition have become internationally famous. Some of these recipes are old friends: Potatoes O'Brien, so well liked that it's justifiably famous outside of Ireland. And so are the elegant American Delmonico Potatoes, named for the restaurant in which it originated. But some recipes have a new look, too. For example, we've included numerous ways to prepare mashed potatoes—each dish with its own name and style. And there are lots more.

French Golden Potato Cake

POMMES ANNA

Perhaps the simplest of the classics, this is also one of the best. The French even named a copper pot after this dish.

Sometimes small white onions are sliced very thinly and layered between the potatoes. But the simpler version is the French favorite. Ours, too!

6 medium-size potatoes (about 2 pounds), peeled
6 tablespoons (¾ stick) butter or margarine, melted
Salt and freshly ground pepper

1. Cut the potatoes into ⅛-inch-thick slices. Place in cold water for 3 hours. Drain and dry the potato slices with a cloth towel.
2. Generously butter a deep glass casserole, 8 inches in diameter. Line the bottom of the casserole with a circular layer of overlapping potato slices; do the same on the sides to form a shell. Layer the remaining slices (they need not be so carefully arranged), spooning a little melted butter or margarine over each. Lightly salt and pepper each layer.
3. Bake, uncovered, in a preheated 400°F oven for 1¼ hours, or until the potatoes are tender and the slices lining the dish are golden brown. Remove the dish from the oven and let rest for 10 minutes.
4. Loosen the sides with a knife and invert onto a hot serving dish. The potatoes should look like a golden cake.

Serves 4

Parisian Potato Balls

6 medium-size potatoes (about 2 pounds), peeled and cut into balls with a melon ball cutter
5 tablespoons butter or margarine
Salt
4 slices lean bacon
2 medium-size onions, chopped
Vegetable oil (optional)
⅛ teaspoon dried tarragon
⅛ teaspoon dried thyme
⅛ teaspoon dried chervil
1 teaspoon chopped fresh parsley

1. Cook the potatoes in boiling salted water for 7 minutes. Drain and dry in the same pan over low heat.
2. In a large frying pan, melt the butter or margarine. Add the potatoes and cook over medium heat until golden, shaking the pan often to prevent sticking. Salt lightly.
3. In another frying pan, cook the bacon until crisp. Drain, dice, and reserve. Save the bacon fat, if desired.
4. Discard two-thirds of the bacon fat, add the onions, and cook until soft (or use vegetable oil). Do not brown the onions.
5. Place the potato balls on a warm serving dish and sprinkle with the onions, bacon, and herbs.

SERVES 6

Château Country Potatoes, "Oeuf" (Egg) Style

8 medium-size baking potatoes (about 2¾ pounds)
1 teaspoon salt
4 tablespoons (½ stick) butter or margarine, melted

1. Peel and quarter the potatoes. Trim the sharp edges so the pieces look like small eggs.
2. In a saucepan, cover the potato pieces with cold water. Add the salt, bring to a boil, cook briefly, then remove from heat. Drain, then dry in the same pan over low heat.
3. Transfer the potatoes to a shallow, buttered baking dish and baste with the melted butter or margarine.
4. Bake in a preheated 400°F oven, uncovered, for 16 minutes. Turn, baste, then cook for another 15 minutes, or until tender and browned.

Serves 6

French Mashed Potatoes with Cheese

7 medium-size potatoes (about 2¼ pounds)
½ cup heavy cream, stiffly whipped
1 teaspoon salt
½ cup grated Gruyère or Swiss cheese

1. Cook the potatoes in their skins in boiling water over medium heat until tender. Drain. Dry them over low heat in the same pan. Peel and mash. Set aside to cool.

2. In a bowl, blend the cream, salt, and cheese.
3. Mound the mashed potatoes in a baking dish. Spread the whipped cream mixture evenly over and around the top and sides of the potatoes, completely covering them.
4. Bake, uncovered, in a preheated 400°F oven until the cheese melts and the top is golden brown.

SERVES 4

Potatoes and Chicken Romano

This Italian classic is nearly always paired with baked chicken, so we include that recipe, too.

6 chicken thighs
6 chicken drumsticks
5 tablespoons olive oil
2 garlic cloves, halved
2 tablespoons chopped fresh broadleaf parsley, or 1 teaspoon dried basil
1 teaspoon dried oregano
1½ teaspoons salt
½ teaspoon freshly ground pepper
1 cup bread crumbs
Hungarian paprika
6 medium-size potatoes (2 pounds), peeled and quartered lengthwise

1. In a bowl, combine all ingredients except the bread crumbs, paprika, and potatoes. Toss the chicken with the mixture, coating it well. Marinate for 2 hours.
2. Sprinkle the bread crumbs on a sheet of wax paper and

lightly dredge the marinated chicken. Use more crumbs if necessary.
3. Transfer the chicken to a large baking dish and sprinkle with paprika.
4. Dry the potatoes with a paper towel and place in the bowl in which the chicken marinated. Toss well and coat with the oil mixture in the bottom of the bowl. Arrange the potatoes around the chicken. Pour any remaining marinade over all.
5. Bake, uncovered, in a preheated 400°F oven for 20 minutes. Turn the potatoes and the chicken and cook for another 20 minutes, or until the potatoes are tender and the chicken is cooked through.

Serves 6

Gallic Creamed Potatoes

1 cup milk
1 cup half-and-half
2 teaspoons of buttermilk
4 large potatoes (about 1¾ pounds)
1½ teaspoons salt
⅛ teaspoon ground mace

1. Mix together the milk and half-and-half. Add the buttermilk and heat until warm. Let stand at room temperature for 1 hour, or until the mixture thickens.
2. Cook the potatoes in their skins in boiling water over medium heat until tender but still somewhat firm. Drain and dry over low heat in the same pan.
3. Peel and cut the potatoes into ¼-inch-thick slices.

Transfer to a flameproof baking dish or casserole. Cover with the milk mixture, then season with salt and mace.
4. Bring to a simmer on top of the stove, then bake, uncovered, in a preheated 300°F oven until the potatoes have absorbed most of the milk mixture, approximately 30 to 50 minutes.

SERVES 4

Baked Potatoes with Cheese Niçoise

This dish is known by various names, but since we first tasted it in Nice, we honor it with that name.

6 medium-size potatoes (about 2 pounds)
3 tablespoons butter or margarine
1 garlic clove, peeled and slightly crushed
Salt and freshly ground pepper to taste
1 cup grated Gruyère cheese (about 4 ounces)
⅛ teaspoon nutmeg
1½ cups milk

1. Peel the potatoes and cut into ⅛-inch-thick slices. Soak in a bowl of cold water for 2 hours.
2. Butter a shallow baking dish with 2 tablespoons butter or margarine. Rub the buttered dish with the crushed garlic.
3. Drain the potatoes and dry with a kitchen or paper towel.
4. Arrange half the potato slices in one overlapping layer in the dish. Sprinkle with salt, pepper, and half of the cheese. Arrange the remaining potato slices on top of the first layer and sprinkle with salt and pepper.

5. Combine the nutmeg and milk and heat to a simmer. Pour the milk over the potatoes. Sprinkle with the remaining cheese and dot with the remaining butter or margarine.
6. Bake in a preheated 400°F oven for 45 minutes, or until the potatoes are tender, the milk absorbed, and the top golden. If the top starts to brown before the potatoes are cooked, cover loosely with aluminum foil.

Serves 4

An American Favorite: Delmonico Potatoes

6 medium-size potatoes (about 2 pounds)
4 tablespoons (½ stick) butter or margarine
3 tablespoons flour
1½ teaspoons salt
2 cups milk
4 hard-boiled eggs, cut into ¼-inch slices
½ cup grated sharp Cheddar cheese
⅔ cup bread crumbs

1. Cook the potatoes in their skins in a small amount of boiling water for 10 minutes. Drain and dry over low heat in the same pan. Peel and cut into ¼-inch-thick slices.
2. In a saucepan, over medium heat, melt 3 tablespoons butter or margarine. Add the flour, stirring into a smooth paste. Blend in the salt and milk, a little at a time, stirring until thickened. Taste for seasoning.
3. Butter a baking dish and alternate layers of potato slices and egg slices, covering each layer with the sauce and a sprinkle of the cheese. The bottom and top layers should

be potatoes. Scatter the bread crumbs on top and dot with the remaining butter or margarine.
4. Bake, uncovered, in a preheated 350°F oven for 40 to 50 minutes, or until bubbling and browned.

SERVES 6

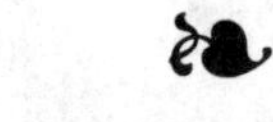

Royal Potatoes

DUCHESSE

These elegant mashed potatoes are sometimes served by the French just as they are, but more often they are used to decorate other dishes and also to rim creamed and cheese entrées. The potatoes are piped through a pastry bag while still warm and formed into any shape desired.

2 eggs
2 tablespoons milk
4 large potatoes (about 1¾ pounds)
1½ teaspoons salt
¼ teaspoon nutmeg
4 tablespoons (½ stick) butter or margarine

1. Beat together the eggs and milk. Set aside.
2. Cook the potatoes in their skins in boiling water over medium heat until tender. Drain and dry over low heat in the same pan.
3. Peel the potatoes and put them through a potato ricer into a bowl. Add salt, nutmeg, and butter or margarine. With an electric beater, whip until velvety smooth.

4. Mix the beaten eggs and milk into the potatoes, whipping until light and fluffy.
5. Form into mounds of any shape or size (or pipe through a pastry bag). Put into a preheated 425°F oven or place under the broiler, watching carefully, and brown lightly.

Serves 6

Oven-Browned French Potatoes

Like many famous dishes, this is simplicity itself. Used exclusively by the French to accompany roast meats, we prefer to serve them with roast veal.

For those who wish to avoid basting the potatoes with the fat from the roast drippings, melt ¼ inch butter or margarine along with olive oil in a casserole. Heat in a preheated 350°F oven. Add the potatoes and cook, covered, for 30 minutes, or until tender, turning the potatoes twice to brown evenly.

6 medium-size potatoes (about 2 pounds)
Roast beef, pork, veal, or chicken

1. Cook the potatoes in their skins in boiling water over medium heat for 12 minutes. Drain and dry over low heat in the same pan. Peel and cut each potato in half.
2. About 45 minutes before the roast is ready, surround it with the potatoes. Turn the potatoes and baste them well with pan drippings at least three times during the final cooking of the meat.

Serves 6

Munich Potato Dumplings

The Germans sometimes split these dumplings and then serve them hot, with melted butter and a sprinkling of toasted bread crumbs. Or they add them to gravied dishes and stews.

4 large baking potatoes (1¾ pounds)
1½ cups flour
1 egg, beaten
1 teaspoon salt

1. Cook the potatoes in their skins in boiling water over medium heat until tender. Drain and dry over low heat in the same pan. Peel and mash. Set aside to cool.
2. In a large bowl, combine the cooled potatoes, flour, egg, and salt, blending well. Knead with your hands into a smooth, elastic dough. If the dough is too soft and moist, add more flour, a small amount at a time, until the dough holds together but is not tough. Shape into dumplings in whatever size desired (we like them to be the size of Ping-Pong balls).
3. With a slotted spoon, lower them into simmering, salted water and cook for 14 minutes. Remove from the water with the slotted spoon and drain well.

MAKES ABOUT 24 DUMPLINGS

Roman Potato Dumplings

GNOCCHI

Those lucky enough to have Italian parents, and others lucky enough to have visited Italy, may have sampled these simple but elegant potato dumplings, called *gnocchi.* We've enjoyed them in Rome, served with a combination of melted butter, cheese, and tomato sauce. We, however, prefer our *gnocchi* with only the butter and cheese.

4 large potatoes (about 1¾ pounds)
Salt
3 egg yolks, lightly beaten
2 to 2½ cups all-purpose flour
6 quarts water
8 tablespoons (1 stick) butter or margarine, melted
1 cup grated Asiago or Parmesan cheese

1. Cook the potatoes in their skins in boiling water over medium heat until tender. Drain. Dry over low heat in the same pan. Peel.
2. Put the hot potatoes through a potato ricer onto a lightly floured pastry board, in a mound.
3. When the riced potatoes have cooled, make a well in the center. Put 1 teaspoon salt and the egg yolks in the well and blend thoroughly. Work in 1½ cups of flour, kneading into a dough. Add additional flour to make a firm, smooth dough that does not stick to your fingers.
4. Divide the dough into 4 parts. Roll each into a long cylinder about ½ inch in diameter. Cut into 1-inch pieces. Gently press the center of each with your thumb.
5. Bring the water to a simmer and add 3 tablespoons salt. Over medium-low heat, simmer a few of the cylinders at

a time, about 5 minutes. Do not crowd. When the dumplings rise to the surface, they are ready.
6. Remove with a slotted spoon, drain well, and transfer to a warm serving dish. Spoon the melted butter or margarine over the *gnocchi* and sprinkle with cheese.

SERVES 8

Burgundian Hash-Brown Potatoes with White Vinegar

We learned the classic and unique technique used in this recipe from our friend and mentor, the famous chef Antoine Gilly.

We like our hash-brown potatoes very crusty and brown. Others prefer them more moist; it's all in the turning and timing.

6 tablespoons (¾ stick) butter or margarine
2 to 3 tablespoons white vinegar
6 medium-size potatoes (about 2 pounds), peeled and diced
1½ teaspoons salt
½ teaspoon freshly ground pepper

1. In a large frying pan, melt the butter or margarine. Stir in the vinegar and the potatoes. Season with salt and pepper.
2. Cook over medium heat. With a spatula, keep turning the potatoes until the desired degree of crustiness is attained. Taste for seasoning.

SERVES 6

Lyonnaise Potatoes

Lyonnaise means it probably originated in the French city of Lyon and that the dish is cooked with onions. This is one of the great potato taste treats.

3 tablespoons butter or margarine
5 medium-size potatoes (1¾ pounds), peeled and thinly sliced
1½ teaspoons salt
½ teaspoon freshly ground pepper
3 medium-size onions, thinly sliced

1. In a deep saucepan or frying pan, over low heat, melt 2 tablespoons butter or margarine. Add the potatoes, salt, and pepper. Cook, covered, for 15 minutes.
2. In a smaller saucepan, heat the remaining butter or margarine and cook the onions until soft, about 10 minutes. Do not brown.
3. Add the onions to the potatoes, tossing well. Cover and cook for 10 minutes, or until the potatoes are tender. Taste for seasoning.

Serves 4 to 6

Potatoes Majordomo

Give the French a potato and their creative cooking talent immediately goes into action. Here is a treat named for a variety of culinary professionals.

6 medium-size potatoes (about 2 pounds)
1 cup half-and-half
1 cup milk
2 tablespoons butter or margarine
½ cup beef broth
¼ teaspoon nutmeg
Pinch of cayenne
Salt to taste
2 tablespoons finely chopped fresh parsley, chives, tarragon, thyme, or basil, or a combination

1. Peel the potatoes and halve them. Over medium-high heat, cook the potatoes in boiling salted water for 10 minutes. Drain and dry over low heat in the same pan. Cut into ¼-inch-thick slices.
2. Combine the half-and-half and milk and heat until hot but not boiling. Set aside.
3. Melt the butter or margarine in a large frying pan. Add the potatoes, the milk mixture, and the remaining ingredients, except the herbs. The liquid should just cover the potatoes. Bring to a boil, cover, and simmer over low heat for 15 minutes, or until the potatoes are almost tender.
4. Remove the cover and cook until sauce thickens. Transfer to a hot serving dish and sprinkle with the fresh herbs.

SERVES 4

O'Brien Potatoes with Onion and Green Pepper

2 tablespoons butter or margarine
1 small onion, finely chopped
1 small green pepper, cored, seeded, and chopped
One 4-ounce can pimientos, drained and cut into strips
Cooking oil
6 medium-size potatoes (about 2 pounds), peeled and diced
Salt and freshly ground pepper to taste

1. In a frying pan, over medium heat, melt the butter or margarine. Add the onion and green pepper and cook until soft. Do not brown. Stir in the pimiento. Set aside.
2. In a large frying pan, heat ½ cup oil. Add the potatoes and cook over medium heat until golden and tender, turning occasionally. Add more oil if necessary. Drain well and season with salt and pepper.
3. Toss the onion mixture and potatoes together over high heat for 1 minute, or until heated through. Taste for seasoning. Serve immediately.

Serves 6

Swiss Grated Potato Fry

RÖSTI

You can grate, cook, and serve each potato cake separately as outlined below or make one large *rösti,* as the Swiss call their national dish. To make one large *rösti,* use a large nonstick frying pan and proceed as follows, using all of the potatoes and 4 tablespoons of butter or margarine.

6 medium-size potatoes (about 2 pounds)
6 tablespoons (¾ stick) butter or margarine
Salt and freshly ground pepper to taste

1. Cook the potatoes in their skins in boiling water for 15 minutes. Peel. Grate the potatoes on the medium blade of a hand grater, so they produce strips approximately ½ by 1 inch.
2. Melt 2 tablespoons butter or margarine in a 6-inch frying pan over medium heat. Add the grated potato strips and mix well, then season with salt and pepper. Flatten and shape the mixture into 6 separate cakes.
3. Lower the heat and cook each cake for about 10 minutes, or until the bottom of each is golden. Shake the pan from time to time or use a spatula to keep the potatoes from sticking.
4. When the bottom of each cake is brown, place a plate over the pan and turn the pan over so the cakes fall out. Slide the cakes back into the frying pan and brown on the other side. Hold the cooked potato cakes in a warm oven until all are done.

SERVES 6

9

Potato Sweets

WE HOPE, AS WITH ANY SATISFYING BOOK, THAT THIS SURPRISE ending will please you. Potato sweets? Yes, and we don't mean sweet potatoes either, as they really aren't potatoes.

Another unique aspect of the potato is that it can be substituted wholly or in part for flour in making cakes, cookies, doughnuts, and pies. Its semisweet mealy goodness melds magnificently with dessert ingredients. And it's economical, too, because you can frequently use leftover mashed potatoes in a variety of these confections.

Not long ago we were invited to a seder. One of the highlights of the meal was a dish of the best macaroon cookies we had ever tasted. The chef told us that they were made with potatoes. Knowing the remarkable alchemy of the potato, which can transform a plain chocolate cake into a moist delight, we didn't doubt his word. Unfortunately, we did not get the recipe.

But we'll try to make it up to you by offering the following repertoire of our favorite potato desserts.

Chocolate Potato Cake

1 cup cold mashed potatoes
2 cups all-purpose flour
1 teaspoon baking soda
1 tablespoon baking powder
8 tablespoons (1 stick) butter or margarine, softened
2 cups sugar
4 eggs
¾ cup buttermilk
1 teaspoon vanilla
1 teaspoon salt
Four 1-ounce squares unsweetened chocolate, melted

1. Place all the ingredients, except the chocolate, in a large bowl. With an electric mixer set at low speed, mix until well blended, occasionally scraping the bowl with a spatula, then beat at medium speed for 4 minutes.
2. Add the chocolate and blend thoroughly.
3. Butter a 13-by-9-inch baking pan; pour in the batter and bake in a preheated 350°F oven for 45 minutes, or until a toothpick pushed into the center comes out clean. Or, bake in three 9-inch layers for 20 minutes, or until the toothpick comes out clean.
4. Let stand for 10 minutes; remove from pan and cool the cake on a wire rack.

MAKES ABOUT 10 TO 12 SERVINGS

Potato Chocolate Drops

1½ cups sifted all-purpose flour
½ teaspoon salt
½ teaspoon baking soda
8 tablespoons (1 stick) butter or margarine
1 cup firmly packed dark brown sugar
½ cup cold mashed potatoes
1 egg, beaten
Two 1-ounce squares unsweetened chocolate, melted
1 teaspoon vanilla
¾ cup buttermilk
½ cup chopped nuts

1. Sift together the flour, salt, and baking soda. Set aside.
2. In a large bowl, cream together the butter or margarine and sugar. Blend in the potatoes, egg, chocolate, and vanilla. Add the flour mixture to the batter alternately with the buttermilk, blending until smooth. Stir in the nuts.
3. Drop well-rounded teaspoonfuls of dough onto greased baking sheets. Bake in a preheated 400°F oven for 10 minutes, or until just crisp.

MAKES ABOUT 3 1/2 DOZEN

Down East Custard Pie

1 medium-size potato (about 5½ ounces)
2 tablespoons butter or margarine
¾ cup sugar
2 egg yolks, beaten
½ cup milk
Juice and grated rind of ½ lemon
2 egg whites, stiffly beaten
9-inch pastry shell, partially cooked

1. Cook the potato in its skin in boiling water over medium heat until tender. Drain and dry over low heat in the same pan. Peel, then mash potato with the butter or margarine, beating until smooth. Cool.
2. In a bowl, combine the cooled potato, sugar, egg yolks, milk, lemon juice, and rind. Blend thoroughly. Fold in the egg whites.
3. Pour the mixture into the pastry shell and bake in a preheated 400°F oven for 25 minutes, or until set.

Serves 6

Potato-Frosted Cake

2 medium-size potatoes (¾ pound)
One 18½-ounce package yellow cake mix
4 tablespoons (½ stick) butter or margarine, at room temperature
Three 3-ounce packages cream cheese, softened

¾ cup sugar
2 teaspoons vanilla
1½ cups walnut halves

1. Cook the potatoes in their skins in boiling water over medium heat until tender. Drain. Dry them over low heat in the same pan. Peel and mash.
2. Bake the cake according to package directions.
3. In a bowl, whip the potatoes, butter or margarine, cream cheese, sugar, and vanilla into a smooth mixture.
4. Evenly spread the potato frosting on the top and sides of the cake. Decorate with the walnuts.

SERVES 10 TO 12

Potato–Molasses Cookies

3 medium-size potatoes (about 1 pound)
2 cups all-purpose flour
2 teaspoons baking powder
½ teaspoon baking soda
½ teaspoon ground ginger
½ teaspoon ground cinnamon
½ teaspoon salt
½ cup dark molasses
8 tablespoons (1 stick) butter or margarine
⅓ cup firmly packed light brown sugar
1 cup chopped walnuts
Confectioners' sugar

1. Cook the potatoes in their skins in boiling water over medium heat until tender. Drain. Dry them over low heat in the same pan. Peel and mash.

2. In a large bowl, sift together the flour, baking powder, soda, ginger, cinnamon, and salt. Set aside.
3. In a double boiler set over hot water, combine the molasses and the butter or margarine. Beat until heated through. Pour into a bowl and beat in the brown sugar. Add the sifted dry ingredients and mix well. Blend in the potatoes until the mixture is smooth. Stir in the walnuts.
4. Drop the batter from a spoon onto a buttered baking sheet and bake in a preheated 375°F oven for about 10 minutes.
5. Sprinkle with confectioners' sugar.

MAKES ABOUT 50 COOKIES

Maine Devil's Food Cake

2 small to medium-size potatoes (about ½ pound)
2 cups sifted cake flour
1 tablespoon baking powder
¼ teaspoon salt
½ cup milk
Four 1-ounce squares unsweetened chocolate
½ pound (2 sticks) butter or margarine
2 cups sugar
4 eggs, separated
1½ teaspoons vanilla
Frosting

1. Cook the potatoes in their skins in boiling water over medium heat until tender. Drain. Dry them over low heat in the same pan. Peel and mash. Keep hot.
2. In a bowl, sift together the flour, baking powder, and salt. Set aside.
3. In a double boiler set over hot water, heat the milk and

chocolate together, stirring well until the chocolate melts. Remove from the heat. Stir in the potatoes, blending well.
4. In a large bowl, cream the butter or margarine and 1¾ cups sugar until light and fluffy. Blend in the potato-chocolate mixture, then add the egg yolks, mixing well. Gradually stir in the sifted dry ingredients. Add the vanilla and blend until you have a smooth batter.
5. Beat egg whites until stiff, then gradually add the remaining ¼ cup of sugar. Fold the egg whites into the cake batter. Pour the batter into three 8-inch layer cake pans lined with buttered wax paper.
6. Bake in a preheated 350°F oven for 30 minutes, or until a toothpick inserted in the center comes out clean.
7. Cool slightly in pans, invert onto a rack, and remove the wax paper.
8. When cooled, spread your favorite frosting between each layer and over the top and sides.

SERVES 10 TO 12

Potato Orange Cake

This cake is surprisingly light and exactly the right flavor and texture to serve with homemade ice cream. The taste of orange is subtle.

4 eggs
1 cup sugar
1 teaspoon baking powder
½ cup potato starch (available in supermarkets)
½ teaspoon salt
2 tablespoons freshly squeezed orange juice
Grated rind of half an orange

1. In a bowl, whip the eggs until thick and smooth, then beat in the sugar until the batter makes a ribbon when dropped from the beaters. Sift in the baking powder and potato starch; add the salt and blend well. Thoroughly mix in the orange juice and rind.
2. Butter a 9-inch cake pan. Cut a circle of wax paper for the bottom and strips for the sides of the cake pan. Line it with the wax paper, then butter the wax paper. Pour in the cake batter.
3. Bake in a preheated 325°F oven for 15 minutes. Turn the heat up to 350°F and bake another 15 minutes, or until set. Turn out on a rack, remove the paper, and cool.

Serves 4 to 6

Potato Pecan Snowballs

8 tablespoons (1 stick) butter or margarine, softened
1 cup confectioners' sugar
¼ cup cold mashed potatoes
2 tablespoons milk
1 teaspoon vanilla
¼ teaspoon salt
1¾ cups sifted all-purpose flour
1 cup chopped pecans

1. In a large bowl, cream together the butter or margarine and ½ cup of the confectioners' sugar. Add the mashed potatoes, milk, vanilla, and salt, blending thoroughly. Using a wooden spoon, stir in the flour and pecans. If necessary, add a small amount of additional milk; the consistency should be that of pie crust dough.

2. Shape the dough into 1-inch balls.
3. Bake on greased baking sheets in a preheated 350°F oven for about 20 minutes.
4. Cool slightly, then roll the cookies in remaining ½ cup of confectioners' sugar.

MAKES ABOUT 3 DOZEN

Potato Torte with Orange Icing

3 large potatoes (about 1¼ pounds)
2 cups sifted all-purpose flour
2½ teaspoons baking powder
½ teaspoon ground cinnamon
⅔ cup half-and-half
Five 1-ounce squares unsweetened chocolate
2½ cups sugar
¾ pound (3 sticks) butter or margarine, softened
5 eggs, separated
1½ teaspoons vanilla
¼ cup orange liqueur
1½ cups chopped almonds
2 tablespoons grated orange rind
Orange Icing (recipe follows)

1. Cook potatoes in boiling water over medium heat until tender. Drain. Dry them over low heat in same pan. Peel. Put the potatoes through a potato ricer or food mill. Set aside.
2. Sift together the flour, baking powder, and cinnamon.
3. In a double boiler set over hot water, heat the half-and-half and chocolate, stirring until the chocolate melts.

4. In a large bowl, cream the sugar and butter or margarine. Beat in the egg yolks, one at a time. Beat in the potatoes, then the chocolate-half-and-half mixture. Beat in the vanilla, liqueur, and flour mixture. Stir in the almonds and orange rind. (The mixture should be smooth and well blended.) In a separate bowl, beat the egg whites until stiff. Fold the egg whites into the batter.
5. Pour the batter into an unbuttered 10-inch springform pan. Bake in a preheated 350°F oven for 1¼ hours, or until a toothpick inserted in the center comes out clean.
6. Cool in the pan. Remove from pan and cool on a rack. Spread with orange icing.

Serves 10 to 12

Orange Icing

¼ cup orange juice
1 tablespoon lemon juice
1½ cups sugar
½ teaspoon grated orange rind
2 egg whites

In the top of a double boiler, beat all the ingredients with a wire whisk until well blended. Over rapidly boiling water, constantly beat for 6 minutes, or until the icing is of a spreadable consistency.

Makes about 2 cups

INDEX